The
Pocket
Therapist

The
Pocket
Therapist

An Emotional
Survival Kit

With a Foreword by Ronald Pies, MD,
Clinical Professor of Psychiatry,
Tufts University School of Medicine

Therese J. Borchard

**CENTER
STREET**

NEW YORK   BOSTON   NASHVILLE

To the best of my ability, I have re-created events, locales, people, and organizations from my memories of them. In order to maintain the anonymity of others, in some instances, I have changed the names of individuals and places, and the details of events.

Center Street
Hachette Book Group
237 Park Avenue
New York, NY 10017
www.centerstreet.com

Center Street is a division of Hachette Book Group, Inc.
The Center Street name and logo are trademarks of Hachette Book Group, Inc.

Printed in the United States of America

First Edition: April 2010

10 9 8 7 6 5 4 3 2 1

Library of Congress Cataloging-in-Publication Data

Borchard, Therese Johnson.
    The pocket therapist : an emotional survival kit / Therese J. Borchard.—
1st ed.
        p. cm.
    ISBN 978-1-59995-299-4
  1. Encouragement.   2. Motivation (Psychology)   3. Stress
(Psychology)   I. Title.
    BF637.E53B67 2010
    158.1—dc22

                                                        2009044984

For my therapist, of course.
And for Mike Leach, the wisest person I know.

Contents

Foreword

That great repository of spiritual wisdom, the Talmud, asks, "Who is wise?" and answers by stating, "The person who learns from everyone." In her new book *The Pocket Therapist,* Therese Borchard shows that she has taken this Talmudic teaching to heart. As she notes in her introduction, she has collected nuggets of wisdom not only from her own therapeutic journey, but also from her husband, family, friends, and even "...the loud guy who was simultaneously eating a hot dog and shouting to the players the other day at the navy baseball game."

To her credit, Therese Borchard does not hold herself forth as an expert in mental health treatment, or as one claiming that merely reading a book—however helpful or profound—can serve as a substitute for professional counseling and treatment. Rather, having grown and profited from her therapeutic odyssey, Ms. Borchard presents the reader with her "sanity file"—the "...tricks, techniques, and sound bites I use between my therapy sessions."

While Ms. Borchard would be too modest to compare her work to some of the world's great spiritual traditions, many of her deceptively simple strategies reflect a deep spiritual wisdom. For example, when she advises, "You can't sit around and wait for the storm to be over. You have to learn how to dance in the rain," she brings to mind a wonderful saying from the Buddhist master Lama Zopa Rinpoche: "We should learn to love problems, like ice cream." Similarly, when Ms. Borchard advises, "Catch the snowball (and toss it back)," she reminds us of what the Stoic philosopher Seneca taught us: "Every trouble that may come our way presses harder on the one who has turned tail and is giving ground."

Ms. Borchard is clearly familiar with many spiritual teachings found in both Western and Eastern traditions, and makes good use of them in her book. But *The Pocket Therapist* is not a textbook of theology or philosophy, nor does it read like one. This is a book of honest self-examination and hard-fought, practical wisdom. Ms. Borchard writes in a breezy, relaxed, and often humorous style that draws the reader in from the very first page. At the same time, her self-disclosures can often be brutally honest, as when she writes, "... I can be so blind to my own attempts at disguising self-destructive behavior in a web of lies and rationalizations." Many readers struggling with their emotional pain will know they have found an empathic and knowledgeable guide in Therese Borchard, as when she writes:

> ... one of the final steps in healing our wounded inner child is learning how to stay with our loneliness: not running away from it or rushing into some activity as a kind of anesthesia. God, does that hurt: staying with the pain of unfulfilled love, expectations, and aspirations. And yet, letting the loneliness come and go as it wants, exactly how our neighborhood dog did when I was ten, is, I suspect, the single most liberating step in my recovery from depression and anxiety.

In many ways, *The Pocket Therapist* is a kind of field guide to getting by in the world—a world in which we often face cruelty, disappointment, and adversity. Therese Borchard has given us a treasure trove of wise parables and shrewd insights, all aimed at helping us deal with the "slings and arrows" of life, while being kind and good to ourselves and others. This is much more than many high-priced therapists deliver!

In the book of Proverbs (4:7), we are told, "Wisdom is the principal thing; therefore get wisdom: and with all thy getting get understanding." I believe that the reader will be well served by following Therese Borchard in her courageous quest for "the getting of wisdom."

—Ronald Pies, MD

Dr. Pies is professor of psychiatry at SUNY Upstate Medical University, where he is also lecturer on bioethics and humanities; he is also clinical professor of psychiatry at Tufts University School of Medicine and editor in chief of Psychiatric Times. *Dr. Pies is the author of* Everything Has Two Handles: The Stoic's Guide to the Art of Living.

Introduction

I'm guessing that you are too broke or busy to go to therapy. Or maybe you do see a shrink, but it's never enough. You wish you had some emotional CliffsNotes to carry with you in case something really bad happens...because you know it's coming... eventually.

If you nodded, smirked, or sighed, look no longer!

The pocket therapist is here!

It's for people who are a tad fragile, like myself, but much more interesting than the folks who never experience doubt, panic, anxiety, sadness, confusion, insecurity, or a day sponsored by Kleenex.

I have saved you oodles of time and mucho money by merely organizing all of *my* therapy notes into a compact little volume that you can carry in your pocket in case you run into the person who gets his giggles and kicks from pressing your TURN ME INTO A BITCH button.

Yep, just for you, I paid a visit to the Ark of the Covenant: a mammoth plastic bin in my garage that stores fifteen journals of notes from more than twelve years (i.e., six hundred hours) of therapy, two binders full of get-ahold-of-yourself tips I learned in the psych ward, and a fat folder of inspirational transcripts compiled from my twenty-one years of attending practically every kind of support group held on this planet.

Then I got even more ambitious. I asked readers on a few different websites—Beliefnet.com, Psych Central, and The Huffington Post—to tell me the most important lesson they learned in therapy.

What a response!

I plucked the gems from those answers and added them to the Ark. Plus any nuggets I have collected in other places: from my swami-mentor Mike Leach; my UPS guy, Dave; the woman who gave birth to me and my sisters; my wise friends like Priscilla, Ann, Michelle, and Beatriz; my husband; a few favorite authors; and the loud guy who was simultaneously eating a hot dog and shouting to the players the other day at the navy baseball game.

As I pored over my scribbled darlings and the advice from others, I said to the Ark, "You are holy, indeed…and it's time I share you."

Why?

I have a feeling a few of my pearls might apply to you. One or two might even spare you some suffering. At the very least, you'll be comforted to know that your distorted thoughts are hardly unique.

It's true that some paragraphs contradict others. You expected that from a bipolar chick, yes? The variety of quips and philosophies I compiled is meant to cover an assortment of moods. Because some days sanity means going easy on yourself—letting yourself cry for two hours as you consume the box of Godiva dark chocolates you bought for your husband—while, at other times, recovery entails getting off your lazy butt and jogging the four miles you promised your personal trainer you would.

And a small confession: I have no real qualifications as mental health expert. I don't have a PhD in psychology, an MD in psychiatry, or any experience as a licensed social worker. However, I *have* scored almost perfectly on the DSM-IV, aka the shrink's manual: I was able to check off most of the diagnoses included in the book! And because of my high aptitude for neurosis, I've become quite creative and resourceful in how I manage this muddled mind.

That's really what this book is: my sanity file...all the tricks, techniques, and sound bites I use between my therapy sessions. These emotional CliffsNotes work for me.

I sincerely hope they work for you, too.

At least until your next therapy session.

The
Pocket
Therapist

1

Count to four

BREATHING IS THE foundation of sanity because it is the way we provide our brain and every other vital organ in our body with the oxygen needed to survive. Breathing also eliminates toxins from our systems.

There are hundreds of techniques for deep breathing, but one of the simplest and most effective ones that I learned in the psych ward is the "Four Step" method:

1. Breathe in slowly to a count of four.
2. Hold the breath for a count of four.
3. Exhale slowly through pursed lips to a count of four.
4. Rest for a count of four (without taking any breaths).
5. Take two normal breaths.
6. Start over again with number 1.

If you get real ambitious, try this: Place your tongue on the roof of your mouth just behind your front teeth. Breathe in slowly through your nose as you count to five. Hold your breath as you count to seven. Then exhale slowly as you count to eight. Put your hands on your abdomen so that you can feel it rise as you inhale.

2

Dance in the rain

MY MOM ONCE told me, "You can't sit around and wait for the storm to be over. You have to learn how to dance in the rain." That's especially true when you're dealing with a chronic illness, and I toss all mood disorders into that category. If you waited until you felt good to go on a bike ride with your daughter or to a happy hour with girlfriends or (some couples really do this) to a quiet dinner with your husband, then your photo album would be pretty empty. Whenever I'm tempted to postpone an event until I have better brain chemistry, I try to do the Macarena instead. Or the polka. Or maybe a waltz.

3

Keep showing up

MY RUNNING COACH told me that if I wanted to run a marathon, all I had to do was to show up at practice. In sweats, not in heels. And the guys who had been sober for double digits said it, too: "Keep showing up to these meetings, and you won't drink."

Success is 99 percent perspiration, even as I'd like it at times to be a result of luck or fate, or some no-brainer thing. Alas, most great achievements—and chasing sanity day in and day out is an act of nobility deserving of a Purple Heart—are accumulated moments of bravery and perseverance gone mostly unnoticed. It's the stuff of every day. Henry Wadsworth Longfellow was right: "The heights of great men reached and kept were not attained by sudden flight. But they, while their companions slept, were toiling upwards in the night."

Wake up to prayer

I'M NOT TALKING about reciting the Stations of the Cross on your knees or praying the rosary in the back of church with the over-eighty crowd on their way to an early-bird special. I mean the process of "waking up to God" that Benedictine Brother David Steindl-Rast writes about, or that Barbara Brown Taylor describes in her book *An Altar in the World:*

> When I look up from feeding the outside dogs to see the full moon coming up through the bare trees like the wide iris of God's own eye—when I feel the beam of it enter my busy heart straight through the zipper of my fleece jacket and fill me full of light—I am in prayer.

5

Don't waste fourteen good days

A GOOD FRIEND once told me that during the two weeks she was awaiting the test results that would determine whether or not she had lymphoma, she said to herself: "Self, it's no use worrying during these fourteen days, because if the results are negative, you will have wasted fourteen good days. And, Self (are you still listening???), if the results are positive, you will also have wasted fourteen good days. Both ways you lose."

6

See with the heart

ONE OF MY very favorite quotes is from Antoine de Saint-Exupéry's *The Little Prince:* "It is only with the heart that one can see rightly; what is essential is invisible to the eye."

Every time I throw myself into a tizzy because things aren't going as expected, or as I projected on my Excel spreadsheet for the year 2020, I have to remind myself that I'm looking with the wrong instrument or organ: I need to go back and tell my heart to get some guts and speak up to my head because it's starting to listen to my eyes again.

For example, when I'm lost in the details—grumpy as hell about having to peddle cans of popcorn, tubs of cookie dough, fifty subscriptions to *People* magazine, or whatever else the school has managed to push on us parents—I miss the expression of wonder on my son's face when he discovers the magic of capitalism...that by knocking on fifty-six doors and begging for money, he has, essentially, won himself a set of tickets to the Orioles game.

Writes Rabbi Harold Kushner: "If you concentrate on finding what is good in every situation, you will discover that your life will suddenly be filled with gratitude."

7

Change the locks

THIS IS A way of taking back control.

Of your thoughts.

Of your brain.

Of your life.

On a piece of paper, draw an oval—it's an oval office—and in the oval, write "Me, the conscious self," because you are the president of Yourself, a nation currently under siege. Now draw a bunch of hallways connected to that oval office. Other people and their opinions travel down those hallways. Most often they arrive at the door to the oval office and enter. The locks on the doorways into these passages are on the outside, giving the people control over when and how often they visit with their opinions and beliefs.

You want to reverse those locks, so that only you have control over who (or what) visits you, how long, and how often.

If you are in a vulnerable place—feeling like your depression is all your fault, and you are a pathetic human being for not being able to pick yourself up by your bootstraps—you might want to lock the doorway to the librarian woman with the tight bun and high-collared blouse who asks you if you truly *want* to get better, implying, of course, that you are willing yourself to stay sick because you're getting so much attention and because fantasizing about death is so much fun. Yes, the witch who depletes your self-esteem by telling you that your suffering is all in your imagination can stay behind her locked door.

The guy with the long-stemmed roses? He can come in and visit you all he wants.

Call a board meeting

SUPPOSE YOU HAVE an important decision to make, and your thoughts are jumbled and muddled—like your living room after you've hosted a playgroup of 15 four-year-olds with ADHD and poor manners. You're confused. You don't know what to do.

Imagine yourself as the CEO of a Fortune 500 company (SerenityNow.com?) who has just called a board meeting. Each voice or thought or opinion has an opportunity to plead its case before you. Once all the perspectives have been heard, you can make your decision.

For example, the woman who doesn't know whether or not to pursue a better-paying but more demanding job needs to call a meeting in her boardroom. She must consider the opinion of the person testifying that she has a low threshold for stress based on her last job. She should hear from the man who says her home life is currently in turmoil and requires some extra attention from her. She ought to listen to the person testifies that her spending habits might factor into the equation. She even needs to listen to the control freak throwing out eighty-five reasons why she is underperforming in her current position and would most likely suck at every other job, too. Then, after processing all the opinions of her board of directors, this CEO makes her final decision.

Come to think of it, the procedure mimics the way the wimps, loners, and losers are voted off *Survivor*.

9

Do it anyway

MAYBE IT'S BECAUSE I live less than a mile from the United States Naval Academy, but there exists within my brain's limbic system—the body's emotional center—a drill sergeant who yells orders in the same fashion as the company officers at the academy.

And that's not all bad.

Because sometimes all I need is a little motivation—plus maybe the threat of something bad happening—to get me out interviewing different doctors, researching why too much of the hormone prolactin makes you cry and lactate (simultaneously!), finding out why my lips have turned a pretty violet shade, looking up all my medication side effects... to see if I come across anything like "propensity to stuff your face and gain twenty pounds," reading up on the benefits of vitamin D and omega-3 fatty acids, trying a different recovery path.

So I apply to my health the same rule that I abide by on my runs around the academy: No stopping until I've run the first mile, which is always the hardest.

This means I can't throw up my arms in defeat at my leaking aortic valve until I've made an appointment with the best cardiologist in my area and researched my valve regurgitation with the persistence and resolve of a midshipman studying for his final exams. I can't relinquish control of my pituitary tumor—and resign myself to a life of nausea and dizziness caused by a medication—until I've met with at least ten different endocrinologists to discuss all my options.

And I can't give up on sanity until I've found the right psychiatrist, therapist, and med combination; added the right foods and vitamins to my diet; cut out the crack-cocaine fix in the morning (only kidding); experimented with a dozen or so relaxation and deep-breathing techniques; forgiven all of my enemies (tried to anyway); studied the brains of people who wake up happy; and tried every other technique and tool in my recovery program.

10

Send it anyway

"DO IT ANYWAY" also means "Send it anyway"...you know, the manuscript you're sure is worse than an engineer's memoir, the proposal that you are positive will get rejected, the self-introduction to the editor whom you are certain doesn't give a damn about your mission to educate six billion people about mental illness.

Send all those things, because, as my hero Helen Keller once wrote, "Avoiding danger is no safer in the long run than outright exposure. Life is either a daring adventure, or nothing."

That's right. Go ahead and dare.

11

Love them anyway

AND FINALLY, "DO it anyway" applied to relationships means that you need only concern yourself about your side of the friendship, marriage, or golf foursome.

In the 1960s, author Kent Keith came up with the ten principles that he calls the Paradoxical Commandments. The first one says, "People are illogical, unreasonable, and self-centered. Love them anyway." This pertains to persons blessed with good brain biochemistry, and to those who aren't.

So when your mother has just given up smoking and drinking in the same week, you must not cancel that trip you planned to go see her, even as you are mighty tempted to bail. Definitely arrange some "day trips" (or exit strategies) during your time with her. Possibly bring some armor, like a few unflattering photos of her you can threaten to upload onto Facebook. But you must love her—withdrawal symptoms and all.

12

Keep saying yes

I BELIEVE THAT a person's first yes—the initial commitment to stop drinking, to pursue help for depression, to start therapy, to begin taking Metamucil—is always the hardest, and that each subsequent yes after that gets easier. But a person is never done. All your life you have to continue nodding, or gesturing in some way that indicates an affirmative...that you're throwing yourself into the process for a 2nd, 3rd, or 697th round.

Because you're never really cured.

But it's okay, because if you're like me, something will have clicked during your first yes, and your life will take on a meaning of its own, one that the psychic you hired at the beach failed to mention, one not included in your projections for the year 2087—a meaning that Swedish diplomat and Christian mystic Dag Hammarskjöld writes about when he says:

> I don't know Who—or what—put the question. I don't know when it was put. I don't even remember answering. But at some moment I did answer Yes to Someone—or Something—and from that hour I was certain that existence is meaningful and that, therefore, my life, in self-surrender, had a goal.

13

And keep saying no

JUST AS IMPORTANT as saying yes is saying no.

If you're unable to utter this consonant–vowel combination, then practice this paragraph several times in front of a mirror:

> You know, I'd love to help you out by hosting an Arbonne cosmetics party, but my schedule is so crammed right now with the kids' lacrosse and soccer, and with my therapy and learning good boundaries—rehearsing script after script on how to say no tactfully—that I simply can't fit it in at this time. I'm sure that the products are unparalleled in quality...just like the Longaberger basket I bought at the last party for a bargain price of three hundred dollars. Try someone else?

Stir the oatmeal

IN HIS BOOK *We: Understanding the Psychology of Romantic Love,* Robert A. Johnson distinguishes human love from romantic love. When we yearn for a passionate romance full of dopamine highs (the rush you get from cocaine and infatuation), we are often blinded to the precious, committed love that is with us every day, the "stirring-the-oatmeal" love. Johnson writes:

> Stirring oatmeal is a humble act—not exciting or thrilling. But it symbolizes a relatedness that brings love down to earth. It represents a willingness to share ordinary human life, to find meaning in the simple, unromantic tasks: earning a living, living within a budget, putting out the garbage, feeding the baby in the middle of the night. To "stir the oatmeal" means to find the relatedness, the value, even the beauty, in simple and ordinary things, not to eternally demand a cosmic drama, an entertainment, or an extraordinary intensity in everything.

I take this concept one step farther. Whenever I'm tempted to choose a more exhilarating or intoxicating path—be it posting a blog about Britney Spears's mental health that will guarantee nice traffic numbers but makes me feel a tad cheap or going on an afternoon talk show that might help my career but hurt my home life—and get fooled into thinking that the glitter will stay shiny forever, I think about the oatmeal.

And I go back to stirring it.

As a recovering addict, this is one of the hardest parts of my recovery . . . to forgo the high, and to continue upon the true but sometimes boring path to freedom and peace.

15

Pick a pace

AS A RUNNER, I know how important it is to pick a pace and stay consistent. I used to run with a group of eight-minute milers, hoping that their speed would somehow rub off on me. The result? I rarely finished the course because I was out of breath, not to mention the harm I did to my body: tearing muscles and damaging tissue.

The same is true about the workplace...and life in general. For three years, I've been trying to keep up with other bloggers who have profiles on Twitter, Facebook, and MySpace, who know how to gracefully navigate the social networking world, who scan two dozen RSS feeds a day and therefore can link back to the major health news stories of the day, who belong to the right professional organizations, and who are abreast of appropriate search engine optimization tools that can grow traffic.

But after a few bad reports from my endocrinologist, cardiologist, and psychiatrist...which are just a few of my doctors... I realized that I'm simply not made of the stuff that they are. As a highly sensitive person—the kind of creature who gets a nervous tic every time she hears the word *Twitter*—I require maybe three times the downtime of an average non-highly-sensitive person. Too much online chatter is toxic for me.

So I scaled back to my ten-minute mile, to my sometimes embarrassingly poky pace.

It might not win me a Webby Award, but it will keep me from pulling too many muscles.

16

Read the signs

YOU KNOW THOSE bad reports I mentioned in my last point, from my endocrinologist, cardiologist, and psychiatrist? I interpret those as signs. That I'm not doing something right, or taking enough breaks for myself.

Here are a few signs I see regularly: STOP; SLOW DOWN; PROCEED CAUTIOUSLY OR NOT AT ALL; LOOK FOR CHILDREN, ESPECIALLY YOURS; CAUTION: JUDGMENTAL RELATIVE AHEAD; DANGER: TRUST ME ON THIS ONE, YOU DON'T WANT TO GO THERE; I SAID STAY OUT! ARE YOU DEAF?; ANNOYING MOTHER ON BOARD; ENTER IF YOU WANT MORE STRESS IN YOUR LIFE.

The Wall Street Journal ran an astute piece by Health Journal columnist Melinda Beck about why it's so important that we listen to what our bodies are telling us. Melinda writes: "The body speaks volumes about what ails it—from obvious warnings like a fever that accompanies an infection to subtle clues like losing hair on the toes, which can be an early sign of vascular disease."

It's taken me a l-o-n-g time, approximately fifteen thousand days, to learn this important lesson. Now I no longer ignore the heart palpitations. They mean I need to chill the hell out. If my fingers and toes and lips turn purple, as they often do with

Raynaud's phenomenon, I consider my stress level. And if my sleep is interrupted for too many nights, I start making changes to my daily routine so that I don't have to drink five large cups of espresso to stay awake.

Moreover, I imagine my living organs as good buddies of mine taking a road trip with me. Every half hour or so, I'll ask them (my brain, heart, liver): "You guys okay? Anyone need to stop for a while and get some rest? Or am I free to crank out a few books, an iPhone application, a few different blogs, and possibly a radio show?"

If they start throwing tantrums like my kids, I know it's time to slow down or hit a rest station. Or to start paying better attention to the signs in my life.

Put on some training wheels

I DON'T KNOW about you, but I never could have raced off on a two-wheeler without first mastering my four-wheeler. In fact, tragic was the day the training-wheel fairy landed at my home and took off with my two little wheels. I still mourn them. Which is why I use a similar system when the task before me becomes too big or too tall.

Take the system that Al Gore created...the Internet. When I receive an e-mail in my in-box, I feel pressured to respond immediately because I am a stage-four people-pleaser. I *used* to stop what I was working on, read it, and respond. That was until responding to e-mail began to consume my day. When I was unable to finish my projects during working hours, I stayed up late to work, which caused another set of problems soon to be discussed.

I decided to try on a handy, dandy set of training wheels, in the form of an automated response. It said this: "I will have lim-ited access to my e-mail for a while, so while I appreciate your writing to me, I may not be able to respond. Thank you for your understanding."

The result? I didn't feel guilty for not responding, and I could better weed out the important e-mails from those that I could discard. I left the automated response on for two weeks...long enough for my people-pleasing brain to catch on that people don't really care if they don't hear back from me. Duh, they are too busy worrying about themselves.

18

Keep your sponges separate

THE OTHER DAY my husband, Eric, caught me cleaning our bathroom sink with the same sponge I used on our toilets. He took the sponge out of my hand and said, "We do not cross-contaminate in this house."

I didn't think it mattered one iota since I had loaded the thing with bacteria killers. But then it made me think of the comment by one of my readers: "Their boo-boos are not your boo-boos." And I understood the deeper philosophy of the sponges.

When I try to console a friend of mine who is having marital problems, I don't have to absorb her troubles and start doubting my own marriage. Our worlds are separate. Just as I don't have to absorb all of my son's hurt when he has a bad day at school or someone was mean to him at lacrosse practice. Although I know I'll always ache when my kids suffer—or when a friend is going through a rough patch in her marriage—I can use different sponges. In fact, it's best if I don't cross-contaminate.

Be nearsighted

MY DAUGHTER, KATHERINE, is very farsighted. Her adorable Coke-bottle glasses correct her vision well enough for her to be able to color fairies, bead necklaces, and watch *SpongeBob SquarePants* on the tube. However, you take away the glasses and she panics.

Hyperopia, the technical term for farsightedness, is an inability to focus on near objects.

Although I don't wear glasses or need contact lenses, I totally understand this vision problem because I have great difficulty seeing the things that are right before my eyes. Instead I concentrate on signs a hundred feet away. I take a project, a goal, a dream, and I view it twenty years away.

Not surprising, then, I get overwhelmed before I even start.

So, as a cognitive-behavioral exercise, I picture myself wearing Katherine's Coke-bottle glasses and try to focus on something that's less than three feet from me. I take a few steps around the base of the mountain I'm trying to climb, or slice off a mere piece of the task I want to accomplish...like recognizing and untwisting *one* of 2,345 distorted thoughts in my head, or attempting *three minutes* versus *three hours* of mindful meditation, or saying no to just *one thing* that I don't want to do but feel like I should because I love that word, *should*, so much.

Forget about all that stuff in the distance, I tell myself, *and focus on the fairies.*

20

Don't go to a hardware store for tomatoes

I DON'T THINK I've ever left a bakery infuriated that they didn't have any hamburger meat, or left a butcher shop disappointed they didn't stock any cucumbers.

But I have done exactly that in so many of my relationships.

I invested my heart over and over again into a friendship that couldn't nurture me in the way I needed. I was determined to find unconditional love with a relative who was more interested in his golf game than in my report cards. Continually, I'd walk to the well, hoping that I might draw a few spoonfuls of water, only to retract a parched bucket.

"Love me, please, just love me," I'd beg the person who was incapable of loving me back.

Now I'm getting smarter. For a confidence boost, I don't write to a gal who delights in belittling me. To feel safe and loved, I don't call up my former boss who hated me or the ex-boyfriend who fancied my friends more than me.

I try my best to go to the bakery for bread.

Don't fret, because you can't unlearn it

MY THERAPIST SWEARS to me that you can't unlearn your progress.

And I'm holding her to it.

She says that even though you have a day or week or year where you flop on building better personal boundaries, or silencing the inner critic, or identifying and replacing the old tapes, you still have all the right stuff inside. You haven't lost any of it.

Nada.

Man, is that comforting in the hours I know my footprints are going in the wrong direction, when I seem incapable of making myself turn around toward healing, when I fret about losing it all—the knowledge, the insights, the discipline that I procured in my recent past—as my strides reverse.

She says your progress is there, stuck in your neural passageways along with instructions on how to ride a bike, even though the dusty thing has been stored in your garage for ten years or more.

So, though we may feel like we're spinning around in circles, lacking the gravity needed to pull us in a certain direction, we're really just learning more. We're exploring…as T. S. Eliot so beautifully said: "We shall not cease from exploration, and the end of all our exploring will be to arrive where we started and know the place for the first time."

Team up!

WE CAN LEARN a lot from geese…aside from techniques on how to crap on the right people.

Did you know that by flying in a V-formation, these creatures not only move faster but can also fly for longer amounts of time and much more efficiently than if they go it alone? In fact, the whole flock adds at least 71 percent greater flying range than if each bird decides to do a solo act. Because each goose in formation provides lifting power for the one behind it.

And when a goose gets sick or is wounded, does the geese group desert the poor guy? Nope. Two of his geese buddies fall out of formation to be with him until he is healthy enough to fly again or until he dies. At that point, they either try to catch up with their original group, or they find another formation.

It's similar to the buddy system I had to abide by back in Girl Scouts. None of us was allowed to go pee in the middle of the night or dart off to the campfire without our buddy. My counselors were not pleased with me when they learned that my buddy had apparently rolled out of our tent in the middle of the night, down a wooded hill, and almost into the creek. Like I had anything to do with that.

Teaming up is useful on many levels.

For one, it makes you accountable. When you have to report to someone, you lower your percentage of cheating by 60 percent, or something like that. Especially if you're a people-pleaser like me. You want to be good, and get a badge or checkmark or whatever the hell they're passing out, so make sure someone is passing out such reviews.

Also, there is power in numbers, which is why the geese system is used in many different capacities today: in the workplace to ensure quality control and promote better morale; in 12-step groups to foster support and mentorship; in exercise programs to get your butt outside on a dark, wintry morning when you'd rather enjoy coffee and sweet rolls with your walking partner.

Get up eight times

THERE IS A wonderful Japanese proverb that says, "Fall seven times, stand up eight." I often think of that quote when confronting challenge number 7,654 for the day, as well as the Buddhist saying, "If we are facing in the right direction, all we have to do is keep on walking." And finally, Mary Anne Radmacher once wrote: "Courage doesn't always roar. Sometimes courage is the quiet voice at the end of the day saying, 'I will try again tomorrow.'"

24

Get your tense right

IN SUPPORT GROUP meetings, I often heard people say, "If you've got one foot in the past, and one in the future, you are going potty on the present." I agree with that line of reasoning, but find myself straddled too often. Nothing about staying in the moment comes naturally.

My regrets cover everything I could possibly have to feel guilty about—from making my mom's day hellish as a colicky newborn, to a second ago, when a bad thought crossed my mind as a happy family waved to me from their yacht. They all live in the past. My anxiety and endless worry about what might happen next belong in the future: My kids could give birth to colicky babies and expect me to babysit, or marry into an annoyingly perfect family who waves to strangers from their yacht.

The present? Not much to fret about there...if I define the present as this very second: my sitting in a coffee shop devouring a warm chocolate-chip macaroon as I listen to Josh Groban's "O Holy Night" and proofread this book. And that's the point, I guess. So I'm trying very hard to follow the words of Buddhist Thich Nhat Hanh:

When you are washing the dishes, washing the dishes must be the most important thing in your life. Just as when you're drinking tea, drinking tea must be the most important thing in your life...Each act must be carried out in mindfulness. Each act is a rite, a ceremony.

25

Catch the snowball
(and toss it back)

A FEW WEEKS ago, I took my son, David, to a navy baseball game. It was the fourth inning and navy was losing, 9–2. A navy guy gets up to bat and hits a double, steals a base, and after the next hit is able to run home. Next thing you know, the bases are loaded and *wham!*, the batter hits a home run.

"That's right, that's right," one of the parents behind me yelled. "Change the momentum."

"Isn't it wild that just one run can alter the energy of the game?" another parent said to the guy yelling behind me.

I thought back to July of last summer, when I couldn't stop crying for a few days. I was scheduled to go to New York for an interview with a magazine and wondered if I should cancel. I went and got through the interview as best I could, escaping afterward to St. Pat's Cathedral, where I continued to sob.

But then that night I went out with some friends and laughed harder than I had in a very long time—they were all telling St. Peter jokes, but the kind you wouldn't find in a Catholic manual—and I felt the momentum shift. In that healing laughter, I knew I was on the mend.

I explained this to a friend of mine who was there that evening, and he said, "Isn't it great when we can catch the snowball and throw it back in the right direction?"

I guess that's what happened.

Somewhere in between the calamari and Buffalo wings, I caught my snowball, before it was too heavy to lift…before I would need the intervention of my doctor or a medication adjustment.

When I can—and there are plenty of times I simply can't, I admit that up front—I try to catch the snowball, to nip my anxiety in its bud…to shift my energy from the problem to the solution, from the infirmity to the remedy, from disorder to good health.

26

Celebrate your mistakes

ALL RIGHT, *CELEBRATE* is an awfully strong word. So then let's start with *accept* your mistakes. I'm not suggesting that you brag about them. Don't make them again, if you can help it. And absolutely do not post them on your Facebook page.

But I do think each big blunder deserves a round of toasts. Or at least a moment of silence and reflection. Because almost all of them teach us precious lessons that can't be acquired by success.

The embarrassment, humiliation, and self-disgust caused by mistakes are all tools with which to unearth the gold, much like the tale that Victor Parachin tells in his book *Eastern Wisdom for Western Minds* about the two men who climbed a tall mountain to speak to a renowned spiritual teacher. Writes Parachin:

> Bowing humbly, they asked the question which had driven them to the teacher:
> "Master, how do we become wise?"
> The teacher, who was in meditation, did not answer immediately. Finally, after a lengthy pause, he responded: "By making good choices."
> "But teacher, how do we make good choices?" they asked almost in unison.

"From experience," said the teacher.

"And how do we get experience?" they asked.

"Bad choices," said the smiling spiritual master.

For example, had I not been medicated on three anti-psychotics at one time, crossed my eyes, and fell into my bowl of cereal at breakfast one morning, I wouldn't think to advise you to interview a psychiatrist much like you would a nanny, to do your own research, and to never, ever yield your authority to someone just because he has the right initials after his name. In fact, take away all my mistakes, and this book would be cut down to about four pages.

Poof! There goes my material.

Just as Leonard Cohen writes in his song "Anthem," the crack is how the light gets in. Or, as Anne Lamott puts it, "In holes and lostness, I can pick up the light of small ordinary progress."

Bribe yourself

A SO-CALLED PARENTING expert whom I read last week claimed that bribing your kid was an example of irresponsible and inefficient parenting. I suspect that the same man sits in his quiet and tidy little office cranking out advice like that while either his wife or his nanny is home changing diapers and doling out time-outs.

Let's face it. Bribing is one of the most effective tools to get anyone—your kid, your stubborn mother, your golden retriever, or yourself—to do something.

My running coach used this brilliant method to train me to run eighteen miles. Before our run, he hid Jolly Ranchers along our route, every two miles. So he'd say to me when I wanted to stop, "In another half mile, you get a treat! Come on, you can do it!" And like a rat spotting a half-eaten hot dog, I'd run to the candy.

You want to make sure you do something? Bribe yourself along the way: at the one-fourth mark, one-half mark, and three-quarters mark.

Be selective, be sincere

I USED TO collect friends like baseball cards.

Visit my Facebook page and you'll see what I mean. I thought that I would look popular and successful if I had more than six hundred friends, so I went click-crazy and befriended friends of friends just for the hell of it. Until I realized I could no longer access the news and statuses of the people I really cared about because it would take too long to sort through details—Joe popped a zit on his way to work today!—of the pimple poppers I don't know from Adam. Short of closing my account and building a new profile, I have no way of getting back to my core peeps.

This is metaphoric, of course, and made me go back and read Anne Morrow Lindbergh's words on friendship in her classic, *Gift from the Sea*:

> I shall ask into my shell only those friends with whom I can be completely honest. I find I am shedding hypocrisy in human relationships. What a rest that will be! The most exhausting thing in life, I have discovered, is being insincere.

The most exhausting thing in life is being insincere. As a stage-four people-pleaser, I know that it's the source of much of my fatigue. Each day, I try to chip away at the artificial layers protecting my heart. I'm certainly not there yet, but I have begun the journey.

Outside of Facebook, that is.

29

Invite the bell

IN HIS BOOK *Touching Peace*, Thich Nhat Hanh describes the big bell in his native village temple in Vietnam. When it sounded, all the villagers stopped what they were doing and practiced mindfulness...they became present to the moment. The Buddhist master writes:

> At Plum Village, the community where I live in France... every time we hear the bell, we go back to ourselves and enjoy our breathing. When we breathe in, we say, silently, "Listen, listen," and when we breathe out, we say, "This wonderful sound brings me back to my true home."

The equivalent for me is my Serenity Prayer key chain.

I hear it jingling exactly when I need to be reminded of the prayer's wisdom. Like when I'm ten minutes late to David's school because a little person forgot his lunch and a pea-brained driver in front of me won't let me get over to the right lane. I'll hear the clank of my key chain and remember that there are some things in life that I can't change—they fall into the first category of the prayer—and that I'd best leave the demonic automobile in front of me alone.

30

Take good notes

ONE DEFINITION OF *insanity*, and I'd throw in *suffering*, is doing the same thing over and over again, each time expecting different results.

It's so easy to see this pattern in others: "David, Scotch tape isn't going to fix the hole in your lacrosse stick"; or "Jane, waltzing around the pool this summer in a Brazilian-cut bathing suit is not going to transform your jerk of a boyfriend into a decent fella." But I can be so blind to my own attempts at disguising self-destructive behavior in a web of lies and rationalizations.

That's why, when I'm in enough pain, I write everything down—so I can read for myself exactly how I felt after I had coffee with the person who was more interested in my publishing contacts than in my health, or after a phone call with the relative who enjoys pressing my bitchy buttons, or after two weeks on a Hershey–Starbucks diet.

Maybe it's the journalist in me, but the case for breaking a certain addiction, or stopping a behavior contributing to depression, is much stronger once you can read the evidence provided from the past.

31

First forgive

MOTHER TERESA ONCE said, "Whatever our religion, we know that if we really want to love, we must first learn to forgive before anything else."

My best friend, Beatriz, taught me that same lesson fifteen years ago when I read aloud to her on the phone the letter I wanted to send my dad: a list of all the important events in my life that he hadn't showed up for and why that was wrong. Granted, I had good reason to be hurt, and it may have been appropriate to send the letter.

But it wouldn't have helped me love him any better.

"I don't think that letter is going to do anything but make him feel guiltier than he already feels, and then keep you that much more out of his life," my very wise friend told me. "Why not make a list of all the things you love about him? Why not forgive him for the mistakes in the past? Why not tell him that you love him so much and want to have a better relationship with him?"

So I did that.

I told him all of that.

And he cried like a baby, and embraced me in a gentle way

I had yet to experience by my father. He also apologized, with undeniable sincerity, for some of his immature and selfish choices throughout the years. As I did.

And then I had three more months to love him before he died.

32

Catch your breath

OPRAH WINFREY EXPLAINED in her commencement address to Wellesley College that it wasn't until she got demoted as an on-air anchorwoman and thrown into the talk-show world that she discovered her true calling.

"The first day I was on the air doing my first talk show back in 1978, it felt like breathing, which is what your true passion should feel like. It should be so natural to you."

It felt like breathing.

I love that. Because writing my blog, Beyond Blue, does feel like breathing... on many days.

I dig for the raw guts and I pretend there are no such things as embarrassment and mistakes—that there's been a recall on all forms of perfectionism—and that each and every reader will appreciate what I have to say, so that no hate mail will have to be read.

I simply take a deep breath and let myself escape unto the page.

Think about a world where everyone followed Oprah's lead and turned their "failures" into opportunities to find their true calling and passion—just so long as it didn't involve public humiliation, of course.

33

Choose a mantra

ACCORDING TO WIKIPEDIA, a *mantra* is "a sound, syllable, word, or group of words that are considered capable of creating transformation." The tradition started in India and was adopted by most of the Eastern religions, but the concept of words possessing creative power can be found in the Gospel of John, too: "In the beginning was the Word, and the Word was made flesh."

All I know is that repeating one word or four words really calms me down. Like Valium does.

My mantras change depending on how desperate I am. Some of my favorites are: "I am okay." "Peace." "I am enough." "I have enough." "Love them." "I will get better." "God, be with me." "Take this from me." "Hello??? Anyone up there??? What the hell are you doing?"

34

Make a self-esteem file and read it

WHAT IS A self-esteem file? The first thing that I would grab—okay, after the kids—if our house were to catch on fire: a simple manila folder containing letters I commissioned from folks on why they like me, hang out with me, even *admire* me. Because I'm not one of those people who can simply look into the mirror every morning and say, "I'm good enough, I'm smart enough, and gosh darn it, people like me!"

The year my self-confidence plummeted like a submarine to below seawater, my therapist told me to go home and list ten of my strengths as a starting point to acquire some self-esteem.

I was unable to do that.

I wrote "thick fingernails" and "a well-proportioned nose" and then I ran out of things to say. So she instructed me to ask four of my closest friends to list ten strengths of mine.

My friend Mike said I was a loyal friend, that I had a big heart and I wore it on my sleeve. Beatriz said she admired my strength to stay sober during our years at college when the entire campus was drunk. Michelle said I could still make her laugh even when I wanted to take my own life.

I put those letters in a folder and labeled it MY SELF-ESTEEM

FILE. It grows every time a reader tells me that my blog has helped her make it through her day or that my singing video gave her a much-needed laugh.

My critics say this is a stupid technique to acquire shallow self-esteem. But you have to start somewhere on the ladder to self-confidence and self-acceptance. And the appraisals inside my noggin are pretty pitiful. So the letters give me courage to put myself out there one more day and see what I get back.

35

Learn how to talk

MOST PEOPLE SPEAK their first word at about eight months old. If you're an adult child of an alcoholic, you said your first difficult word at about age eighty. Because every time you opened your trap to voice your opinion growing up, you got either shot down or the silent treatment. I don't know which I preferred. So my mouth didn't really learn to say anything but "sorry" until I miraculously landed in therapy.

I suppose I could call my weekly counseling sessions "speech therapy," because that's where I learned how to articulate the hard stuff: to ever-so-*tactfully* (not a strong suit of mine) express my feelings, concerns, resentments, opinions... all the things I kept inside for the first quarter of my life.

Now I know how to use "I statements" ("I'm sorry that YOU CAN'T HEAR A BLOODY WORD I'M SAYING, IDIOT") and other tools taught in Communication 101 for Persons Raised in Dysfunctional Homes.

Quit the acrobatics

ACROBATICS?

Yeah.

Like *leaping* to judgments, and *jumping* to conclusions. These things happen in the air, and the goal is to stay on the ground... where you have evidence for opinions and facts supporting judgments. Because without the evidence and the facts, you're dealing with assumptions, and we all know that assumptions are the termites of relationships.

They eat away at the connective tissue between two people.

"Don't make assumptions" is the third agreement of don Miguel Ruiz's classic book *The Four Agreements.* He writes: "All the sadness and drama you have lived in your life was rooted in making assumptions and taking things personally."

If you want more sadness and drama in your life, continue to leap and jump. Hell, try a backflip. If not, try your best to stay grounded.

Don't take it personally

JUST AS CRUCIAL as don Miguel Ruiz's third agreement is his second: "Don't take anything personally."

The first time I read it, I laughed out loud.

"Dude," I said to his mug shot on the back cover, "why don't you just tell me to go on a vegetable diet for the rest of my life?"

But I do think if you can pull this one off, you spare yourself *a lot* of suffering, not to mention free up oodles of brain capacity.

I like to think of my emotions as the opposite of a tax return: The less I claim, the better off I am. So when I think that a friend of mine is upset with me by the way she is acting—not returning my phone calls, blowing me off at school pickup or soccer practice, giving me the bird—but she hasn't said anything to me, I don't need to worry about it.

Not until she spills her can of whoop-ass all over me do I have to worry my neurotic little head about what's going on in her limbic system.

And guess what? Even then, I still don't have to claim it.

That's entirely up to me!

Ruiz writes: "Even when a situation seems so personal, even if others insult you directly, it has nothing to do with you. What they say, what they do, and the opinions they give are according to the agreements in their own minds."

So when I get a really harsh e-mail or fifty that say something like, "Your blog is stupid. You're annoying. Your videos suck," I read Ruiz's chapter on the second agreement and say to myself, "Your blog may be stupid, you may be annoying, and your videos may very well suck, but you got the final say on that. Not them."

38

Go in, not out

HERE'S A PIECE of wisdom I've learned from the most spiritual guy on earth, my metaphysical hero of sorts, Mike Leach: You, and you alone, are responsible for your happiness.

No one person, place, or thing can do the job for you.

I remember how relieved I was the first time he said that to me...as if my fate didn't depend on picking the winning lotto number, or right relationship, or proper career, or on growing up in the perfect nuclear family where two stable, profanity-free parents would gather their emotionally nurtured, well-adjusted offspring around a cozy fire to discuss Homer's *Iliad* and *Odyssey*...that I could be happy even in the midst of dysfunction.

Yah!

Because there's lots of that where I live.

But the second part of this adage requires substantial perspiration and a love relationship with dirt. Because you have to dig deep, burrow into the compartments of your soul, and meet who is there. If she's standing there naked with sagging breasts and a butt full of cellulite—with a pathetic vocabulary and low SAT scores—you have to accept and love her anyway.

I remind myself to "go in, not out" at least sixty-seven times a day, because my first inclination is always to grab for something to make me happy. It's easier to collect than to dig. But at the end of the day, you're sitting in the midst of a bunch of crap that you've amassed, feeling empty with one more job to do: de-cluttering.

39

Go through it, not around it

ONE MORE NAVIGATING tip to ensure that you don't wander around in the desert for forty days like Moses did because he was like every other man...afraid to ask for directions: It's almost always better to go through the heart of an issue than around it.

Because no shortcut is without its share of construction.

If you disagree with me, spend a year in Chicago. There I learned that it is possible to repair every street at the same time, making it damn near impossible to arrive at work on time.

During my two suicidal years, my therapist must have pulled out her GPS navigating system two or three times a session.

"Through it, not around it," she'd repeat.

I appreciate her logic now that I'm on the other side.

Because if I had looped around some of the issues that were tearing me apart inside, then I would have bumped into them somewhere in my future, or be trapped in a traffic circle like Clark Griswold in *National Lampoon's European Vacation*. By going through the intense pain, I eventually surfaced as a stronger person ready to tackle problems head-on. And the pain eventually lost its stranglehold over me.

Stay with the loneliness

ACCORDING TO JOHN Bradshaw, best-selling author of *Home Coming,* one of the final steps in healing our wounded inner child is learning how to stay with our loneliness: not running away from it or rushing into some activity as a kind of anesthesia.

God, does that hurt: staying with the pain of unfulfilled love, expectations, and aspirations. And yet, letting the loneliness come and go as it wants, exactly how our neighborhood dog did when I was ten, is, I suspect, the single most liberating step in my recovery from depression and anxiety.

I read the following paragraph from Henri Nouwen every morning as part of my daily meditation because in his words lies my escape from slavery:

> It is not easy to stay with your loneliness. The temptation is to nurse your pain or to escape into fantasies about people [or places or things] who will take it away. But when you can acknowledge your loneliness in a safe, contained place, you make your pain available for God's healing.

Solicit the pros

I ONCE MADE the mistake of soliciting marriage advice from a woman who had been divorced four times. That was, until Eric shared this important nugget with me: "When you want to play better golf, you should watch a Tiger Woods tape, not the man hacking balls into the parking lot at the driving range. And when you want to write better prose, don't ask the ladies at a Tupperware party for those tips. Seek the experts."

Now I know better than to ask a friend who has never popped a Klonopin to tell me how to manage anxiety, or to ask the woman who has never worked outside the home for secrets on juggling home and career. I think I might even refrain from quizzing the married woman registered on eHarmony for pointers on avoiding an extramarital affair.

Be picky from whom you solicit counsel.

With exception to me, of course.

42

Think short term

THINK LONG TERM WHEN you're chatting with your financial adviser. Think short term when you feel like hell. That's right. Take it anywhere from twenty-four hours to twenty-four minutes to twenty-four seconds—depending on how bad you feel—and repeat over and over again these four words: *This too shall pass.*

Coupled with deep breathing, the phrase *This too shall pass* is one of the most powerful tools with which I combat anxiety. I will repeat it as many as a hundred times in five minutes. Without fail, it will help me to adjust my breathing from my chest to my diaphragm. It's a reminder, too, that no feeling or emotion is permanent, even as I try to apply superglue to some. Moreover, everything in this world of ours is transient...which is somewhat of a bummer on the good days, but so much consolation on the bad.

43

Honor your neurosis

I USED TO try to separate my brain into two parts: good (productive) and bad (neurotic). Until I realized that this was simply impossible because the sensitivity that produces so much of my pain is precisely what makes me the compassionate person I am.

The Buddhist nun Pema Chödrön says this:

> Our wisdom is all mixed up with what we call our neurosis. Our brilliance, our juiciness, our spiciness, is all mixed up with our craziness and our confusion, and therefore it doesn't do any good to try to get rid of our so-called negative aspects, because in that process we also get rid of our basic wonderfulness.

Take Disney's Tinker Bell, for example.

She didn't like being a tinker fairy. So she tried to become a water fairy and carry dewdrops to large spiderwebs. Instead, she evaporated all the dewdrops already on the web. So she attempted to become a light fairy and supply all the lightning bugs with their glows, only to accidentally light up her rear end. And then she endeavored to be an animal fairy and help the little birdies learn to fly. But in doing so she attracted a large, nasty hawk who wanted to eat the baby birds.

The sad fairy returned to her workshop and resumed her boring work of fastening widgets and pounding nails and chopping acorns. Until, one day, she stumbled upon a curious collection of metal pieces and parts. Gradually, she began to assemble them into a magical, musical box. And in that moment, she was proud to be a tinker fairy.

Me?

I'm an obsessive-compulsive manic-depressive addict fairy. We can perform all kinds of unique tasks that the water, light, and animal fairies can't. And while I used to frown at all my neuroses, now I am seeing that there are things only I can do. In fact, the French writer Marcel Proust once said that "Everything great in the world comes from neurotics." Yah! That's good news for me!

44

Buy the Tootsie Rolls

MY THERAPIST KEEPS a large bowl of Tootsie Rolls on the table between my couch and her chair. I usually treat myself to two or three on the way out, because sometimes our sessions feel like I've just climbed Mount Everest, or at least burned off six hundred calories.

"You must really like Tootsie Rolls," I said to her the other day upon leaving.

"No, I don't," she responded, "that's why I buy them. Now, if I bought Reese's cups, I'd be in trouble."

I always knew she was smart, my therapist, but that logic put her up there with Albert Einstein and Thomas Edison.

For me, buying Tootsie Rolls means avoiding people, places, and things that will trigger my competitiveness and manic streak...especially workaholics and overachievers. Because I will try to keep up with them, even as I'm out of breath. Then I crash. My family has to pick up the pieces, which puts me in the doghouse. And too many nights in the doghouse leads to depression and anxiety.

For that reason, I don't open an important file that is sent

to me every Monday morning containing my blog traffic numbers, which of my posts were most popular, which sites are
linking to me, and which key terms generate the most traffic.
I'm sure it's all interesting stuff, but I can't go there...it's a big
Reese's cup.

Unplug

IN HER BOOK *Finding the Deep River Within*, Abby Seixas has a name for the constant state of busyness in America: "the disease of a-thousand-things-to-do." Here are the symptoms: rushing, rushing some more, cussing while rushing, never having enough time, misplacing your car keys, cussing while trying to find your car keys, being interrupted while cussing about your lost car keys.

And the biggest casualty, in my opinion, of this disease?

Mean people get *meaner* and crazy people get *crazier*. (I am, of course, in the second group.)

So what do I do about my illness?

Unplug.

Twice a year, for at least ten days.

It's like a silent retreat with screaming kids.

Despite the deafening yelps from the little people in my surroundings, the absence of all the online chatter in those days does wonders for my mental health and for my soul. I find myself (there you are!) after looking for her for five months, and I have a good chat with myself about my values and priorities, none of which say that I need to accomplish 5,987 things in two hours in order to be accepted and loved. Sometimes I even emerge from my unplugged session in a delightful mood. That is, before I see the 2,837 e-mails I need to answer.

Peek inside some other homes

I USED TO believe the world comprised two groups of people: the mentally ill and the normal folks. That kind of thinking—an "us" against "them"—contributed to a jaded, bitter, resentful attitude toward my illness.

Why was this done to me? I bemoaned quite often.

One day my blindfold fell off and I began to see all the different kinds of problems in the lives of those around me: the friend who went to wake her baby after naptime and found her dead in the crib, one of those rare statistics of Sudden Infant Death Syndrome; the colleague raising two special-needs kids who will never be able to care for themselves or live independently; the countless mothers who have lost their sons to the war in Iraq.

The more conditions I contract and the more doctors I add to my address book, the more capable I've become of recognizing suffering in everyone's life. No one is immune, even as some pretend to be. It's like the tale that American Buddhist Lama Surya Das tells in his book *Letting Go of the Person You Used to Be:*

> The Buddha was once approached by a grieving mother whose little child had just died. She pleaded with him for a miracle: She begged him to restore the child to her alive

and well. The Buddha listened to the bereaved woman and finally said that he would be able to do what she asked if she could bring him a mustard seed from a home that had never lost anyone to death. The mother traveled far and wide, day after day, trying to find such a home, and of course she couldn't. Finally she returned to the Buddha and said that she had come to realize that death visits everyone. It was a reality she had to accept. And in that acceptance she found strength and consolation.

47

Process heat and suffering like a coffee bean

THERE'S A STORY that goes like this: One day a young woman was whining to her father about how hard life was. She was tired of fighting and struggling. Sounds familiar, right?

He was a chef, so he set out three pots and boiled water in each of them. In the first he placed a carrot, in the second an egg, and in the third some ground coffee beans. After twenty minutes, he turned off the burners. Then he explained how all three reacted differently to the heat. The carrot went in firm, but softened in the boiling water. The egg hardened on the inside. And the coffee beans, well, they actually changed the water.

"When you confront adversity, which one will you be?" he asked his daughter. "The carrot that starts out strong but wilts under pressure? The egg that becomes callous and bitter? Or the coffee bean, which makes something useful, tasty, even beautiful from the boiling water?"

48

Befriend yourself

HAVE YOU EVER wondered how long one of your friends would stick with you if you talked to her the way you shout at yourself?

My therapist calls me on this dichotomy practically every session.

"What would you say to a friend in your shoes?" she'll ask me.

"I'd tell her to be gentle with herself, to eat a pint of Ben & Jerry's, and spend three hours watching Oprah if it made her feel better."

Of course I need not go that far—especially if I don't want to weigh three hundred pounds—to exercise a little kindness to myself. Most of the time, all I have to do is to put away the whip and make myself a friendship bracelet instead.

49

Poke fun at your problems

I THINK RITA Mae Brown had the right attitude when she wrote, "The statistics on sanity are that one out of every four Americans is suffering from some form of mental illness. Think of your three best friends. If they are okay, then it's you." She attempts to have a little fun with a solemn subject.

So should we.

Because laughter relieves stress, reduces pain, boosts our immune systems, and helps us to fight viruses and foreign cells. Plus, it cultivates optimism, that sunny and sometimes-annoying attitude of life that can do wonders for your mood, protecting you from negativity, fear, and panic.

But the most important reason to laugh?

It's fun.

And it surely beats crying, although from ten feet away most people can't tell the difference.

50

Bawl your eyes out

IN A RECENT *New York Times* piece, writer Benedict Carey refers to tears as "emotional perspiration." As an easy crier who sweats a lot, that makes perfect sense. But I'm not ashamed to cry, because tears heal in a variety of different ways.

For one, they remove toxins from our body. Emotional tears (those formed in distress or grief) contain more toxic by-products than tears of irritation, like when you peel an onion, indicating that weeping is surely nature's way of cleansing the heart and mind.

Second, tears elevate mood. Crying lowers a person's manganese level, and the lower the better because overexposure to manganese (whatever it is) can cause anxiety, nervousness, irritability, fatigue, aggression, and the rest of what happens in your brain when you or your spouse are in a foul mood.

Finally, crying is cathartic.

You've felt the same release that I have after a good sob, right?

It's as if your body has been accumulating hurts and resentments and fears over the period of a year, a month, a week, or a half second...until your limbic system runs out of room and then, like a volcano, the toxic gunk spews forth everywhere...

onto your sweater, or a friend's sweater, or a Kleenex, if you're lucky enough to catch them.

That's good! Because the cardiovascular and nervous systems run more smoothly after some emotional perspiration.

51

Sweat

WORKING OUT YOUR distress quite literally—by running, swimming, walking, or kickboxing—is going to give you immediate relief.

On a physiological level.

Because exercise increases the activity of serotonin and/or nor-epinephrine and stimulates brain chemicals that foster growth of nerve cells. In fact, some recent studies have suggested that regular exercise can be just as effective as antidepressants to lift a mood.

And emotionally.

Because by wearing a stylish sweat suit and sneakers, we become the sergeant with a whistle, taking charge of our health and giving orders to our mind and body, even if our limbic system, tummies, and thighs are in sorry shape and curse us for forcing them to move or do a sit-up.

You don't have to be training for a marathon to feel the anti-depressant effects of exercise. Even picking the weeds and watering the flowers have been shown to boost moods. However, I have found kickboxing especially effective because you can visualize the fellow who is responsible for your pain and hi-yah him in the face.

Now, doesn't that feel good?

52

Take a shower

THIS DIRECTIVE NOT only applies to those depressed and anxious persons whose therapists have told them that they smell... you know, like my therapist did a few years ago. But also to folks who need to trick their brain into believing that they feel great!

Taking care of yourself—starting with soaping up your skin and shampooing your hair—is usually a no-brainer when you're feeling good. Not so when getting out of bed feels like completing an Ironman at age eighty-five. But that first effort—of putting your left foot on your bedroom floor followed by the right foot—can thrust the momentum in the right direction, so that your brain starts to follow your body toward good health.

Thus, showering and scrubbing your armpits is one way of "faking it till you make it," and it's been my experience that after you fake serenity and sanity for a few twenty-four hours, your limbic system begins to chill out a tad.

Until your next shower...which is...a day later?

53

Find a mentor

HOW WOULD YOU like to cut your mistakes in half?

Then get a mentor.

Not a role model or a professional adviser—although those can't hurt, either. What you want is a person who can, in the words of author J. R. Parrish, "act like a filter to help you avoid costly mistakes and guide you through the perilous waters of life." Or, as spiritual author Henri Nouwen explains, "keep reminding you of where your deepest desire is being fulfilled... [because] you distrust your own knowledge."

My mentor's primary job is to remind me that I am loved for who I am. I need not accomplish any major feat, win a Pulitzer Prize, or be the most popular blogger on the Internet in order to be loved and accepted. All I have to do is to take a few deep breaths and be my neurotic self. So, as you can imagine—given all my insecurities—my mentor is a very busy man!

54

Start uni-tasking

I REALIZE SOME multitasking is required in our rushed culture. But do we really have to simultaneously cook dinner, talk to Mom, help with homework, and check e-mail? If you were a stellar waiter in your past who could memorize the orders of a dozen tables while entertaining all of them with witty commentary on the fish du jour, maybe you thrive at juggling multiple tasks.

Me? I have trouble snacking on peanuts while making macaroni and cheese. Seriously. Twice while making mac and cheese, I became distracted and dumped the packet of cheese flavoring into the boiling water. (That's not the proper order.)

As a mom who works from home on many different projects, I thought focusing on one responsibility at a time would be impossible until I made myself abide by some simple rules: My computer is off when I'm not working, and my computer stays off in the evening and on weekends. My brain appreciated the new house rules and actually started to relax a bit.

I don't care what the iPhone ads say, I don't need to be in

touch with everyone all the time. Multitasking is too damn stressful for me. So if you think you have fragile chemistry like I do, turn off your CrackBerry and concentrate on the macaroni and cheese. Before you dump a packet of cheese flavoring into boiling water.

55

Carry a blankie

EVERYONE NEEDS A blankie.

Okay, not everyone.

Mentally ill recovering addicts like myself need a blankie, a security object to hold when they get scared or turned around. I need reminders—ideally, 234 of them—to refresh me on goals, promises, and prayers I pledged or recited in the morning with my coffee. And because tattoos are expensive and well, permanent, I go with jewelry, medals, and beads I can hang on to.

Specifically, a medal of St. Therese that I carry in my purse or in my pocket.

My medal gives me consolation. It reminds me that the most important things are sometimes invisible to the eye: like faith, hope, and love. So when I doubt all goodness in the world—and accuse God of a bad creation job—all I have to do is close my eyes and squeeze the medal.

56

Keep a consistent rhythm

I'M NOT TALKING about rap, or your tempo on the drums. I'm referring to your circadian rhythm, the internal biological clock that governs fluctuation in body temperature and the secretion of several hormones, including the evil one, cortisol.

Here is how you establish good rhythm that assists you with the whole sanity thing: You live a boring life.

Sort of.

You have to go to bed at the same time every night, and wake up at the same time. Preferably with the same person. You can't befriend Australians, or if you do, you can't visit them. Because travel, in general, and especially travel to different time zones, will throw off your circadian rhythm. During the fall and winter months, I stare into my HappyLite for an hour a day because, fragile creature that I am, my brain mourns the sunlight that it gets in the spring and summer.

Folks with seasonal affective disorder and bipolar disorder have to be especially careful to prevent disturbances in the circadian rhythm in order to keep their friends and their jobs.

And long-term disruption can actually do mega damage, like messing with the peripheral organs outside the brain, and contributing to or aggravating cardiovascular disease. Chronic disruption of the circadian rhythm can suppress melatonin production, too, which has been shown to increase the risk of cancer.

So I suggest you get yourself an alarm clock and a light box right now.

57

Get off the (legal) drugs

HERE'S THE CATCH-22: The more stressed you are, the more you crave coffee and doughnuts, pizza and Coke. But the more Starbucks, Krispy Kreme, and Big Gulps in your system, the more stressed you become. Because when it's stressed, your body has lower levels of serotonin, which causes your brain to produce cravings for sugar and simple carbohydrates, which primes the beta-endorphin system to want more and more.

The same with caffeine.

It's a powerful drug that affects a number of neurochemicals in your brain, which means it produces withdrawal symptoms that can make you very very very very irritable.

58

Build a guesthouse for your feelings

"THIS *BEING HUMAN* is a guest-house," wrote the thirteenth-century Sufi poet Rumi. "Every morning a new arrival, a joy, a depression, a meanness... Welcome and entertain them all!"

I love that.

Because you can always kick them out!

Let's say feelings are like any other visitors in that, like fish, they smell after three days. You welcome them, set out a cheese plate, learn a thing or two from them—like from which neighborhood of your brain they come from... the childhood-scars region, the obsessive-compulsive vicinity, or the paranoia district—and then after a night or two, you tell them to hit the road.

It's a win–win situation!

59

Imitate an eagle

WHY?

An eagle knows that a storm is approaching long before the storm comes. He will hoist himself way up high and wait for the winds to come. Then, when the storm arrives, he steers his wings so that the wind will raise him up and lift him above the storm. While the squall thunders below, the eagle is gliding above it. He hasn't dodged the storm. He has simply used the fierce winds to lift him higher.

60

Imagine the worst

I KNOW THIS seems wrong—like it would produce even more anxiety. But imagining the worst can actually relieve fear.

For example, when I was hospitalized the second time for severe depression, I was petrified that I would never be able to work again, to write again, to contribute anything to society. I was literally shaking with anxiety, I was so scared of what my illness could do to me.

I called my friend Mike and rattled off to him all my fears.

"Uh-huh," he said. "So what?"

"What do you mean, 'So what'? My life as I know it might be over," I explained.

"Yeah, and so what?" he said. "You can't write. No biggie. You can't work. No biggie. You have your family who loves you and accepts you. You have Vickie and I who love you and accept you. Stay home and watch Oprah all day. I don't care. You'd still have people in your life who love you."

You know what?

He was right.

I went there in my mind: to the worst-case scenario . . . me on disability, hospitalized a few times a year, unable to do so much of what I did before.

And there I was. Still standing. Or lying on the bed.

Sure, life would be different. My family would face challenges. Eric could have a breakdown of his own, joining me for bingo hour in the community room. My kids might wonder why Mom disappears every few months and can't chaperone any of their field trips. But we would all still be leading a full life. A different life, yes, but a life. And I was okay.

Really okay.

61

Negotiate for what you need in a relationship

MIKE ALSO REMINDS me on a regular basis that marriage is about compromise between two givers. He and his wife, Vickie, have a rule that whoever feels more strongly about something—skipping dinner with the country-club snobs, flying south to visit with the hillbilly relatives—gets her way. He told me to try it out in my own relationship.

So when America decided it no longer needed or could afford to build and renovate homes—when the housing market was officially flushed down the toilet with the rest of the economy and practically all architects became unemployed—Eric and I sat down with our budget and crossed off lots of "desired but not necessary" items.

The house, for Eric, was a non-negotiable. His type of living organism requires the space of a three-bedroom house to thrive, whereas I could inhabit a junk closet...as long as there was space and an outlet for my HappyLite. On the other hand, sending the kids to St. Mary's was at the top of my list, as I wanted them to get some religion from a source other than myself, so that they wouldn't associate all things spiritual with "crazy."

So, following Mike's advice, whenever we run up against a situation like our budget, we ask each other one simple question: "What is most important to you?" And, as long as I'm not about to get my period, this system seems to work.

62

Give back

GANDHI ONCE WROTE that "the best way to find yourself is to lose yourself in the service of others." Positive psychologists like University of Pennsylvania's Martin Seligman and Dan Baker, PhD, director of the Life Enhancement Program at Canyon Ranch, believe that a sense of purpose—committing oneself to a noble mission—and acts of altruism are strong antidotes to depression.

When I'm in pain, the only guaranteed antidote to my suffering is to box up all of my feelings, sort them, and then try to find a use for them. Because when you turn your attention to another person—especially someone who is struggling with the same kind of pain—you forget about yourself for a split second.

And let's face it, on some days that feels like a miracle.

63

Forecast some backsliding

THE PATH TO mental health is an *uneven* process: For every two steps forward, you move one and a half back. But if you know this before you start walking, you'll be less tempted to throw up your arms at the first relapse and say "to hell with it!"

My psychiatrist had to remind me of this lesson every session for about a year, until I reached a stable place.

I'd march into her office cheerful one week—ecstatic to be working again and laughing with my kids—and then, boom! It felt like I was as depressed and anxious as I was back in the psych ward.

I wasn't.

It just felt that way since it happened after two weeks of feeling good, in the same way that fifty degrees feels like summer in January and winter in June.

In one session, Dr. Smith drew a zigzag line to illustrate the typical path of recovery and help me understand that I wasn't pedaling in reverse, I was merely getting comfortable as a driver; and that recovering from severe depression, or making any kind of progress toward good health, is never perfectly symmetrical.

64

Give Amy a bottle

I NOW KNOW who to blame for my feelings of panic and anxiety...Amy.

It's all her fault.

That's what I call my amygdala, the delinquent cluster of neurons in the limbic system considered by most neurobiologists as the *fear center* of the human body, like the "welcome center" of college campuses, except that instead of providing glossy brochures, Amy doles out panic attacks.

This almond-shaped group of neurons is responsible for making us act like apes, those very hairy creatures from which we've evolved...most of us anyway. Whenever you begin to feel the adrenaline—perhaps, for example, when you open your e-mail to find a thousand messages and among them a Facebook friend request from your ex-boyfriend who smashed your heart like a callous hairy ape—envision the almond neurons, the brat Amy, and warm up a bottle of milk for her.

"Ahhh, there you go. Much better."

65

Make a puppet

HERE'S JUST ONE more exercise to help you respond to the chorus of critics who might be running around singing songs in your head. Sad songs. Mean songs. Critical songs, like "You're no good, You're no good, You're no good, Baby you're no good." (Thank you, Linda Ronstadt.)

For the self-critic who follows me around all day just like a nitpicking, fault-finding boss, I have made a puppet.

Yes, a puppet.

I simply cut out my photo and glued it on a brown paper bag. And now every time the inner critic pipes up with "You're such an idiot," or "This is kindergarten homework and you can't figure it out?"—I'll take out the puppet, put her on my hand, and scold her: "I've had plenty of criticism for one day! That's enough out of you!"

66

Designate a no-bash zone

BETWEEN THE AFTERNOON hours of four thirty and six, and/or whenever I am seated in the rocking chair Eric bought for me after I bore his first child, I am not allowed to insult myself.

Zippo.

Nada.

Nil.

This is the time of day when all the processed sugar and red dye from the Superman cupcakes served at one of the birthday parties at my kids' school start to make my life a living hell. As I watch my spirited tykes throw popcorn and baseballs from the kitchen to the living room and play hide-and-seek under our glass end table, I don't blame the sugar and red dye. No, that would be too simple and logical. I condemn myself for the mayhem that's invaded our home. And the neighbors'. And their in-laws'.

However, if I am in my no-bash zone, I am protected from the voice that says that I am at fault somehow, instead of the manufacturers of red dye or whoever baked and served large quantities of processed sugar to minors. And I can't hear the inner critic who is ready to sign me up as the next pathetic mom on an episode of *Nanny 911*, because I was born without the parenting gene. Nope, I can sit back in my no-bash zone and say, "I hereby swear that I did not bake the Superman cupcakes that are responsible for the bizarre behavior at this very moment. So help me God."

I am, for that moment anyway, officially off the hook.

Educate yourself

I'VE NOTICED A direct correlation in my life between educa-
tion and worry. That is, the more I understand something, the
less I fret about it.

For example, the week my cardiologist told me that the tear in
my aortic valve was leaking fluid (regurgitation) and my endocrinologist informed me that my pituitary tumor had grown by
30 percent, I did a panic dance: I called all my friends and family and told them that I was dying, so if they had any last words
for me, they'd better start talking.

A friend urged me to inform myself on both conditions—
exactly as I had done with my bipolar disorder—and the result
was astonishing: I chilled out a bit and removed the automated
e-mail response that said, "In lieu of burial flowers, make a
donation to my poor husband."

The more I read about the endocrine system, pituitary
tumors, and aortic valve regurgitation, the more empowered I
felt to explore better doctors, alternative treatments, and creative
solutions...to take my health back into my own hands again,
which, in turn, lowered my anxiety level by about 80 percent.

Label and replace
the old tapes

IN HIS BOOK *Cutting Loose*, Howard Halpern explains that we all have videotapes of our childhood experiences and feelings recorded in our brain cells. These insecurities and inadequacies—CHILDHOOD PAIN, basically—are often replayed in the present. If we know these tapes are playing, we can stop them from doing any further damage. *And* if we label them correctly, just as we do our Disney movies, we can ensure that we won't make the mistake again—or in the same week anyway.

It's like this... Imagine you're out to dinner at some classy joint with a bunch of colleagues, and then all of a sudden, the lights are dimmed in the restaurant, a flat-screen TV on the wall behind you gets turned on, and your worst childhood nightmare—the time you got the tail end of a chicken bone stuck in your retainer and Susan Herbenicks had to stand up in front of the entire sixth-grade class and administer the Heimlich maneuver to you—is being broadcast for all of the restaurant to see.

"Excuse me for one moment," you might say to your table as you grab your linen napkin from your lap, stand up, and turn off the TV.

That's how I like to think of my old tapes (i.e., "You're weak, pathetic, lazy, and ugly"). "Oops, they're up on the TV! Hold on, guys, let me turn off that piece of technology." If my eyes are trained enough to identify them up there for all to see, I realize how ridiculous it is to play them so many years later, to so many people who don't know anything about me. Alas, I can replace the tapes *pronto* with better ones.

Barbra Streisand anyone?

69

Practice gratitude

GRATITUDE DOESN'T COME easily to this depressive. When my girlfriend sees a half-full glass of fresh milk, I see a half-empty glass of cholesterol-raising, cardiac-arresting agents. And when the kids' school is called off because some road somewhere in our county apparently accumulated half an inch of snow, she thanks God for an opportunity to build snowmen with her kids.

Me? I have a conversation with God, too, but it's much different.

However, I train myself to say thank you more often than is natural for me because I know that gratitude is like broccoli—good for your health in more than one way. According to psychologists like Sonja Lyubomirsky at the University of California–Riverside, keeping a gratitude journal—where you record once a week all the things you have to be grateful for—and other gratitude exercises can increase your energy and relieve pain and fatigue.

So I take my hand of cards and I start counting the winners: I live in a country where I get paid to whine; I have married the most empathetic and caring man in the Western Hemisphere; I have two imaginative children with all of their limbs; and I have a fridge that is currently stocked with dark chocolate.

Yep, I definitely feel better.

70

Say om

I'M NOT TALKING about yoga, although research shows that the regular practice of yoga may raise a person's levels of the neurotransmitter gamma-aminobutyric acid (GABA), thereby making him smile more and cuss less.

I'm referring to omega-3 fatty acids.

Smart people at Harvard Medical School have confirmed that omega-3s make you tolerate mean people, refrain from road rage, and politely inform telemarketers that there are no decision makers at your house. So eat them up in salmon, tuna, sardines, walnuts, canola oil, or flaxseed. Better yet, have capsules shipped to your household like I do. But make sure they meet the doctor-formulated 7:1 EPA (eicosapentaenoic acid) to DHA (docosahexaenoic acid) ratio, or else you have just wasted a lot of money.

So much for not cussing.

71

Anticipate exceptions

A PIECE OF advice from my high school French teacher: Anticipate exceptions!

She was explaining grammar rules for the French articles *le* and *la*: which kinds of nouns each article precedes. *"La will most of the time* precede *these things,"* she said. "Except in *these cases*..."

As soon as my brain would wrap itself around a rule, I'd be hit with another list of exceptions.

So I raised my hand.

"Okay, Mrs. Smith, I understand where you are going with this, but is there any rule in the French grammar that doesn't have like a hundred exceptions??? Is there any rule that is absolute?"

She paused for a minute.

"No," she said with a half smile. "In life, nothing is absolute."

I will always remember that.

Especially when I'm making rules for the kids. "Absolutely no candy before six o'clock. Except when Dad is away and I need to bribe you with Kit Kats and Skittles."

Allow room for accidents

ONE OF THE best lessons my mom ever taught me was to always allow room in my schedule for accidents.

I adhered to her instructions in college.

Whenever I wanted to pack my semester with eighteen credit hours, taking an extra class in Renaissance art because maybe I would meet a sophisticated guy who did more on his weekends than slam cheap beer, I'd remember her advice and drop the class. I never went over fifteen hours, simply to allow room for the unexpected, which always happened.

During my sophomore year of college, my dad contracted a lethal pneumonia that eventually killed him, so I needed the extra time to jaunt back and forth from South Bend, Indiana, to Dayton, Ohio. The next year I descended into a suicidal depression and invested hours in therapy, seminars, self-help literature, and medical research because I wanted to better understand my mood disorder.

Today I often forget my mom's wisdom, and I suffer the consequences. When my flight is delayed by half an hour, I panic because I really needed those extra thirty minutes. I'd already factored them into my frantic schedule. But when I follow her advice—when I write two weeks' worth of blogs and put them in the bank in case I have a day where I can't write—my brain thanks me for putting that much-needed cushion in place.

73

Keep a "success log"

WHEN GETTING OUT of bed was the hardest thing I did each day, my therapist instructed me to record *all* of my accomplishments in a day. So I jotted down things like: "walked the dogs for 15 minutes," "ate half of a bagel," "took a shower," "watched the kids for an hour," "filled out a medical claim for Satan, I mean, our health care insurance provider." Those five accomplishments were part of building a recovery program that would start to include many more accomplishments as I stabilized over time.

It was an important exercise that communicated to my brain that this body–mind–soul engine was headed toward health, *not* despair, helplessness, disability, or death.

I continue to log my successes today.

In fact, I keep a "boundaries notebook," where I write down specific triumphs in my day that involve building better boundaries.

For example, when a friend asks if I can watch her four kids so that she can go grab a massage, haircut, and dinner out with her husband, I no longer reply, "Of course! And let me know if you want me to scrub your toilets and walk your dog, too!"

Those days are over. I simply don't respond, or tell her that I am already engaged at that time (WITH SANITY, THANK YOU VERY MUCH).

74

Get your ZZZs

SLEEP IS CRUCIAL to sanity.

CRUCIAL!!!!!!!!!!

Because sleep disturbances can contribute to, aggravate, and even *cause* mood disorders and a host of other illnesses. Yep. The link between sleep deprivation and psychosis was documented in a 2007 study at Harvard Medical School and the University of California–Berkeley. Using MRI scans, researchers found that sleep deprivation causes a person to become irrational because the brain can't put an emotional event in proper perspective (it has PMS) and is incapable of making an appropriate response.

You see, if you're not sleeping, your brain doesn't have an opportunity to do all the stuff it needs to do without the constant interruption of your thoughts. The brain works night shifts. And when it doesn't get all the work it needs to do done... well, it gets a tad irritable, like you do when you can't get your work done. And it takes it out on you.

Moreover, your circadian rhythm—the internal biological clock that I discussed earlier—is like a high-maintenance houseguest... if you don't give it what it wants, you will suffer the price.

Chronic sleep deprivation, especially, is bad news.

For one, it makes your spouse miserable, because tired folks tend to snap more easily and bite innocent heads off. It can affect your memory ("I'm sorry, dear cousin, what was your name?") and your concentration ("I forget what I was just saying... Oh yes, my concentration... It's bad").

According to one recent study, sleep deprivation can cause a decline in cognitive performance similar to that seen in the intoxicated brain. That's right! Drunks can reason and judge better than you if you've gone too long without getting some ZZZs.

And finally, sleep disturbances make you fat.

Yep.

You eat more when you're tired and stressed. Notice the folks around you snacking on potato chips. Do they look well rested?

See what I mean.

Squeeze in some downtime

THERE IS ANOTHER kind of rest that is almost as crucial to your mental health as sleep: *downtime.*

What is that? I don't have a clue, but my sane friends tell me it's great.

Downtime lives in quadrant II of Stephen Covey's time-management matrix: It's *important* but *not urgent.* So we say "fahget about it." But we really shouldn't "fahget about it," because downtime is our cushion against stress. If your body is without a cushion for too long, the pieces tend to fall apart. Like Humpty Dumpty. And I hate to bear the bad news, but sometimes the doctors can't put you back together again.

Spot distracters

I BELIEVE EVERYONE has a little ADHD in them. Not that we all need to take Ritalin with our orange juice in the morning. But it is so very hard to stay focused: on our work project, on our recovery from *fill in the blank*, on our celery-and-hummus Skinny Bitch diet, on our New Year's resolutions to stop practicing voodoo on our health care insurance providers.

As a freelance writer, I have to manage my own time, which is like sending my dessert-obsessed daughter into a candy store with instructions to pick out a birthday card for Aunt Sue. I lug my laptop to coffeehouses that, for the most part, facilitate my concentration efforts. Which means when I see a woman with a painted butterfly on her cheek climb out of her car with all kinds of paints and balloons and children's books, I know to get the hell out of there and hit a safe zone like the library to work.

The same is true with other distracters in my life.

I no longer entertain everyone's theory on mental illness, especially folks who believe all disease is born from bad thoughts. I no longer attend family functions sponsored by Miller Lite. And for the time being, I avoid blogging conferences and professional associations that will activate a part of my brain that I want fast asleep.

Act as if

I THINK MOST people with mood disorders are deserving of at least one Academy Award in their lifetime: for all those performances in which they pretend they possess normal bio-chemistry and aren't on the verge of a panic attack, nervous breakdown, or massive crying fit.

Me? I'm acting during most of my waking hours. Because when the average mom walks up to me at school pickup and asks, "Hey, what's up?" I don't think it's appropriate to respond: "It's quite a match today. Team NIT (Negative Intrusive Thought) is killing Team PT (Positive Thinking) 15–2, and it's only halftime."

Sometimes I get cocky—and think that I can pull off an Oscar performance anytime—but then I'll run into an extremely com-passionate person who looks me straight into the eyes as she asks me, with utter sincerity, "How are you?" And I'll burst into tears followed by a few good pig snorts.

So I have a bit of practicing I need to do yet.

Nibble on dark chocolate

NOTICE I DIDN'T write "devour" or "inhale," which is, unfortunately, how I eat dark chocolate. But yes, it's true, if you can control yourself in front of a box of Godiva—and if some mean relative or friend hasn't taken a bite out of each piece—then you can enjoy antidepressant benefits by simply stuffing your face.

How is this so?

The technical answer is that dark chocolate contains resveratrol, an antioxidant that can raise your levels of endorphins (natural opiates) and serotonin, which together act like Prozac without the side effect of dry mouth! That's right, an ounce a day keeps the psychiatrist away. Or, well, maybe a few weeks away.

Go ahead, I say...indulge!

79

Fire your inner psychic

YOU THINK YOU'RE psychic, don't you?

Just like the gentleman who read my palm at a wedding and told me, "You will have many lovers, but will live a long and lonely life."

Thanks, dude. Appreciate that.

Or his relative who put his hands on my belly three weeks before I was due with my first kid, and said, "Girl. Yes, absolutely."

Eric and I named *her* David.

I do think some folks have this sixth sense of intuition. They see dead people. Sort of. I'd like to think I am intuitive. But so often I use this gift incorrectly and see things in my crystal ball that simply aren't there. Like that Joe D. hates my guts and he should because how could anyone like me?

My crystal ball often says, "The world hates you because of X, Y, Z." So I say back to the crystal ball: "You don't know squat, you stupid sphere...Go find the spirit of that pseudo-psychic who read my palm at the wedding. Tell him he will live a long and lonely life."

Don't dare compare

THE LAST THING you should do when you're stressed—which I always do when I'm stressed—is look around at other people's supermarket shopping carts loaded with desirables (cake job, family support, balanced brain) and wish you could steal a few items. I grow especially jealous of non-addict friends who can relax with a glass of Chardonnay at dinner or colleagues with moms around the corner who take the kids all day.

But I don't have all the information.

The free mom-babysitter might also have an opinion on every piece of furniture in her daughter's house, and her own spare key to that house so that she can pop in anytime—like when, God forbid, she might try to have sex with her husband or hire somebody else to. The gal who enjoys her wine might be lactose-intolerant, unable to consume large quantities of Ben & Jerry's, poor thing.

If you absolutely must compare, pick a guy worse off than you. Practice Helen Keller's sage advice: "Instead of comparing our lot with that of those who are more fortunate than we are, we should compare it with the lot of the great majority of our fellow men. It then appears that we are among the privileged."

Find someone with bigger problems

I'M NOT GOING Catholic here...indicating that all your tribulations should fly away like colorful helium balloons once you see pictures of starving kids in Cambodia.

No. No. No.

I know what guilt does to the human body after forty years.

I'm just saying that sometimes hearing someone else's set or *sets* of problems can bring you relief.

Take my friend Lee.

Whenever I begin the dangerous descent into the Black Hole of Bile, I will ask Lee to have coffee with me. I ask him, "So... what's going on in your world?" And that's all I really need to say to feel better.

Because Lee is the modern-day Job of the Bible.

Remember? The guy who sounds like a country song, because he lost his wife, house, and truck all in the same day?

Lee will fill me in on his son's latest addiction—the twenty-something-year-old likes to adopt new ones every few weeks to make sure he wins the self-destructive contest; the latest plot by his Cruella de Vil mother-in-law to destroy him; and any progress of his daughter, who is severely mentally and physically handicapped and will never be able to live independently.

Within five minutes of listening to Lee, I'm having another conversation altogether.

With God.

"Thank you so much for not doing that to me. Thank you, God. Don't you ever try that on me. You know I wouldn't be able to handle that, right, God?"

And right then and there, thirty pounds fall off my back because I am so relieved not to be Lee.

Take your time and buy the right pants

THE SISTERHOOD OF the Traveling Pants is an endearing story about four girlfriends and a pair of blue jeans. My pants tale is a little different, but with an important lesson, nonetheless: *Always take the time to do something right.*

A while back, I was forced to get another pair of denims by a friend who could no longer look at the black ink stains on the right pocket of my ratty jeans. She drove me to the mall, dragged me into the Gap, and told me to pick out a pair.

I grabbed the first pair of pants I saw, bought them, and told her that our mission had been accomplished. Except that when I tried on the pair at home, I realized they were a "plumber cut," meaning three-fourths of my crack showed when I bent down to clean up a milk spill on the floor.

"You rushed when you bought those. Didn't you?" asked Eric, exactly the way Mike, my writing mentor, did ten years ago when I handed him four children's books that I had published—cranking out each manuscript in under seven hours.

"You didn't take your time with these and it shows," he told me.

I vowed to myself that I would never make that mistake again.

Umm...I do still rush when under a pressing deadline. But at least now I use a thesaurus so my sentences are longer than four words.

However, when I rush on an important decision in my life—aside from choosing the right words—I have no thesaurus to save me, and sometimes the consequence is a bit more serious than a rear view. I always wish I had taken the extra fifteen minutes to try on the jeans. So that I could clean up spilled milk without worrying about the pervert behind me.

Bring in the engineer

I SUSPECT THERE is a strong correlation between common sense and mechanical abilities.

Engineer-type folks like my architect husband were born with an abundance of logic. When their crushed ice doesn't fall through the freezer dispenser as it should, they open up the ice compartment to see what's jammed.

Me? I keep pressing the ice button twenty-five more times—convinced it will eventually work if I try again (with the right thoughts). When I finally do investigate by opening up the freezer, hundreds of cubes spill out unto the floor.

The same is true with personal problems.

I tend to give a technique, oh, 505 shots to work, at which point I come away exhausted and thoroughly frustrated. The engineer? After two failed attempts, he spends his energy figuring out a better method.

That's what you're aiming for. To stop trying to use your jammed ice-cube maker after two tries and to peek inside the freezer and see what in the hell is keeping the cubes from falling down the chute like they should. Or, if you prefer, learn how to enjoy your beverages at room temperature until your engineer of a husband returns.

84

Get your timing right

IT WAS ONE of those rare mornings when the entire family had managed to make it to church.

We were halfway through the service when six children dressed in white walked up to the altar to be baptized. The priest was pouring water on the forehead of a beautiful six-year-old girl...the church completely silent...when all of a sudden Katherine's Island Princess Barbie starts singing: "Here on this island, the sea says hello! Dolphins are splashing wherever you go!"

I couldn't count the number of rows that glared back at us with disdain, but I'm sure it was a double digit. It reminded me of the prayer service on the Friday after 9/11, when, at the moment of silence, two-month-old David released a very loud bubble of gas.

Ah yes, the importance of timing.

At support groups, I learned the wisdom of HALT: Don't say anything remotely important when you are *hungry, angry, lonely, or tired,* which pretty much covers all of my waking hours. So I've revised it to mean: Keep my trap shut in the car (I'm always nervous), after eight or more hours with the kids (especially in bad weather), and during holidays, when I'm known to binge on sweets and coffee. But, hey, if you're feeling balanced and whole, serene and well rested, talk all you want...just as long as it's not when everyone else is being quiet at a prayer service or baptism.

85

Don't let fear motivate you

A GOOD FRIEND of mine recently considered applying for an executive position at her marketing firm, a step up the managerial ladder from her job. The position paid a higher salary but would require some late nights, weekend work, and would involve more of the administrative tedium that bored her to death.

She procrastinated completing the application, and every time she spoke to me about the job, she was obviously less than enthused.

"If the job requires more time at work and lots of the monotonous work you hate, then why are you applying for it?" I finally asked her.

"Because four people in my department have already applied for it, and if one of them gets the job, I know I'll kick myself for not having applied."

"That's not a good enough reason," I said. "Fear should never be the motivating factor in a decision."

Of course it's much easier to spot the fear in someone else's life. I'm often oblivious to my own panic. But I do think I'm getting better at assessing my motivation for certain behaviors and decisions. If I feel the urge to move in one direction out of trepidation over where the other path might take me, I sit with that intention awhile longer, so that I can tease out the worry and anxiety before I make my decision.

And it's not always the right one.

But I'm hoping the more I can recognize a motivating fear, the more right decisions I'll eventually make.

Dump the bad guilt

AS A CATHOLIC, I have great difficulty deciphering between good guilt and bad guilt.

Guilt is guilt, and it all purifies the soul, right?

In a make-believe world of fairies and goblins, where spirits are all good or all evil, yes. On the Planet Earth, when too much guilt can disable a person from living a productive life, um...NO!

So here's the way my therapist taught me to distinguish between productive and unproductive guilt—which I think she picked up from one of Pastor Paul White's telecasts from Poplar Bluff, Missouri: I label as "convictions" those desires or thoughts coming from a place in my heart that simply wants to love better and be a better person, and I label as "condemnations" those generalized judgments that serve no purpose other than to make me feel worse about myself.

Take my guilt about how much TV my kids watch.

The conviction: *Let's try to limit the TV to no more than two hours a day.*

The condemnation: *Give your kids up for adoption now because Paris Hilton would make a more suitable mother than you.*

You see, the conviction provides some detailed suggestions to help me do better, whereas a condemnation is a statement you might hear yelled out of a trailer followed by the sound of a bottle of liquor tossed into a trash can.

You get the distinction?

Be quiet

HUSH.

Be silent.

If only for three seconds.

Because constant noise and distraction, especially for a "highly sensitive person"—a human being who reaches over-arousal of the nervous system by watching ten minutes of *Dora the Explorer*—can decay the tender places of a soul if you're not careful. Too much staring at a computer monitor, with a combination of Hannah Montana and Mario Kart Wii playing in the background, could impair your judgment...and make you think that buying more Wii games and preteen pop-star crap is a good idea.

Moreover, quiet time returns us to what is true, good, and beautiful...without Xanax! The Trappist monk Thomas Merton wrote:

> In silence we face and admit the gap between the depths of our being, which we consistently ignore, and the surface, which is untrue to our own reality. We recognize the need to be at home with ourselves in order that we may go out to meet others, not just with a mask of affability, but with real commitment and authentic love.

Reel it in

WE ALL KNOW how fast our thoughts can take on a life of their own. A slight hitch in a project becomes an impossible hurdle, a well-intentioned gesture by a friend morphs into a ruthless backstab, and a minor criticism from a colleague turns into a threatening dissertation about your inadequacies—you know, everything that's bad about you and why you shouldn't get out of bed in the morning.

Granted, buried within any rumination are usually kernels of truth. But other parts are way off in fantasyland—with about as much accuracy as there is in a juicy celebrity tabloid story: "Céline Dion Meets ET for Drinks." That's why you need some good friends who will help you separate fact from fiction.

When I call up my friend Mike and tell him my latest loony thoughts, he usually says something like this: "Wow. Reel it in. Reel that baby in... You are way out there this time."

And then we laugh at my wild imagination.

Get back to your senses

MEDITATION CAN APPARENTLY change your brain.

Neuroscientist Richard Davidson of the University of Wisconsin conducted a study whereby the group of people who meditated showed a greater increase in activity in the left prefrontal cortex of the brain—the region associated with happiness—than the nonmeditating group.

But I am somewhat of a meditation and mindfulness moron . . . I don't see myself transcending before this country elects a woman president. When I close my eyes and try to meditate, my thoughts begin a game of Marco Polo, with the amygdala (fear center) blindfolded as Marco, trying to tag all nearby thoughts.

So I usually begin with the senses.

I start with the sense of taste, of course, and head to a coffee shop, where I ask my favorite barista to warm up a chocolate-chip or oatmeal-raisin cookie and make me one of his delicious cappuccinos. With every bite and sip, I pretend I am blindfolded, like my amygdala, and I savor every mouthful, trying to concentrate on nothing but the toga party inside my trap.

Then I will go find some water—the magical oxygen–hydrogen combination that brings me back to the beginnings of life—and I study the movement of the ebb and flow, imagining myself there, in the middle of the Chesapeake Bay on Katherine's little daisy surfboard, rising and falling with the tide.

Then I close my eyes and let the wind play with my hair, giving the breeze my full attention until I go on to the next sense.

The abbreviated version goes like this:

Step one: Stuff your face.
Step two: Think about stuffing your face as you're stuffing your face.
Step three: Be grateful for the food that you're stuffing in your face.
Step four: Stare into space.
Step five: Look happy as you're staring into space.

Try it, my form of meditation.
For this obsessive-compulsive gal, it beats sitting in lotus position on a yoga mat.

Take baby steps

OTHER WAYS OF saying this: *Break the job down. Start small. Tackle one task at a time.*

For example, as I was beginning to ascend out of the abyss of my severe depression, I was overwhelmed by everything—a sinkful of dishes, a menacing diaper, a doctor's appointment. Decision making was especially painful: for me and for the waiter (*Ranch? Italian?...Ranch? Italian?...What would you have if it were your salad?*). And I didn't have a clue as to how to restart my career. Every time I thought about it, I began to shake with anxiety.

My great-aunt Gigi, who had suffered her own nervous break-down at age thirty-five, coached me along the way. "Itsy-bitsy steps," she'd remind me. So I signed up to be a writing tutor at the Naval Academy for three hours a week, just to see if I could manage my emotions for that long.

I succeeded! Except for the morning I burst into tears because I couldn't concentrate long enough to read a midshipman's boring paper about the history of the Tripoli Monument.

Then I asked my editor at the news outlet where I had worked pre-breakdown if I could resume my biweekly column. That step was harder, especially during the weeks when I'd sit at a blank computer screen for an hour or more, waiting for my words to come out from hiding. But I forged on. I continued to write, a little article here and there, which eventually led to Beyond Blue, a leap, but one I was able to take because of the smaller steps that came before it.

91

Build on your strengths

ACCORDING TO POSITIVE psychologist Martin Seligman, the most important step we can take to achieve lasting happiness is to identify our signature strengths and find ways we can use them in meaningful work.

I have used the worksheets provided in David Burns's *Ten Days to Self-Esteem* to do this. I first explored my gifts, like caring about people and wanting to solve their problems, and then listed some possibilities as to how I might use them, either in a profession (Beyond Blue!) or as president of the Bleeding Heart Association, a nonprofit that aims to solve the world's problems without having to ask anyone for money.

This exercise was immensely helpful because it shifted my concentration from the long lists of things I don't do well—domestic tasks like cleaning, cooking, planting, or any activity involving two or more screaming kids—to my strengths. And that gave me hope that there was a use for me in this world even though all of my plants are dead and I can mess up a peanut butter and jelly sandwich.

92

Hang with the winners

PEER PRESSURE NEVER really goes away, you know.

Studies show that married folks hanging out with happy couples are more likely to stay married themselves; that if you surround yourself with optimists, you will end up more positive than if you keep company with a bunch of whiners; and that if your friends eat well, their willpower will rub off on you. In fact, when presented with the dessert option of pumpkin cheesecake, chocolate-raspberry torte, or vanilla crème brûlée, you will instinctively shake your head from side to side.

Human beings unconsciously and consciously mimic the behaviors of those around them, which is why all the women living in Regina Hall at Saint Mary's College my freshman year were on the same menstrual cycle, and, with everyone going through PMS at the same time...well, that explains some of the behavior.

As a recovering alcoholic, I know that you're much more likely to relapse if your pals frequent drug rehabs more than grocery stores, and as a manic depressive, I have learned that staying sane is an easier job if you avoid those who talk doom and gloom, because once the negativity is out there, it's up to me to tell my brain not to dwell on it.

Since that's a big job, I try to hang with the winners.

Hug and hug often

HUGGING IS LIKE spinach: good for your health.

A research study at the University of North Carolina has found that hugging can dramatically lower blood pressure and raise levels of oxytocin, a good hormone (as opposed to cortisol) that helps a person chill out, relax, breast-feed, and orgasm, although not all at the same time. The women in the study who got more hugs from their husbands had much higher levels of oxytocin, and had systolic blood pressure that was 10 mm/Hg lower than women with low oxytocin levels.

But you didn't need to be briefed on all that to believe in the benefit of hugs, right?

Hugs are non-negotiable in our house. They are part of the morning routine, bedtime routine, and you-two-better-make-up-in-the-next-five-minutes routine. They are as necessary as brushing teeth, as healing as aloe vera and Barbie Band-Aids, and more coveted than Klondike bars. And the best news of all? They're free!

Go out and play

I USED TO think that recreation by definition translated into laziness, and that I should be judged by what I produce, not by how I play.

I was a human doing, not a human being.

But then I realized—after a few trips to the psych ward—that I can't produce anything of value unless I've had substantial time in the sandbox or on the swing set.

Recess is just as important for our bodies and brains as homework or learning how to master a new skill or time spent at the office. In fact, recent studies show that a person can become more stress-resistant by adding four to six hours a week of "active leisure." Not watching *Baywatch* or *American Idol*. Something in which you have to do more than work the remote control. Like knitting or fly fishing. Or maybe fantasy football, whatever the hell that is.

How do I play?

Sipping cappuccinos with friends, licking mint-chocolate-chip ice-cream cones with lots of chocolate sprinkles, kayaking through the fingers of the Chesapeake Bay, mountain biking through the woods, swimming in clean pools without Band-Aids floating in the lanes, and running through the stunning campus of the Naval Academy.

Whine (with the right crowd)

NOT EVERYONE CAN tolerate whine. And I do agree that in large doses, the stuff is dangerous...toxic, even. But there is nothing more freeing, empowering, and comforting to me than finding a human being with whom I can be completely forth-right about my pain, a person who can remind me that acknowl-edging my suffering is the first step toward feeling better, and that just because my neighbor might be burning up with a temperature of 102 that doesn't mean my temperature of 101 is insignificant or that I can't gripe about it.

I don't fully understand how gabbing heals—the scientific explanation of why venting does so much good—but I can surely attest to it, and confirm the connection between talking about something and feeling substantial relief.

It's like you're a scared little kid in a lightning storm, and a neighbor, seeing that you're locked out of your house, invites you inside and makes a cup of hot chocolate for you. Actually, maybe the human exchange of the hearts *creates* the thunder-storm, as Martin Buber says: "When two people relate to each other authentically and humanly, God is the electricity that surges between them."

Offer it up

I'M NOT A saint or martyr. I would not be ecstatic to die for Jesus. Especially if the process involved pain.

But when I am suffering and can think of no purpose for my misery, it helps me to remember those in similar situations who are enduring greater agony than I am. So, if I'm cursing the dizziness and nausea that I'm experiencing as side effects of my pituitary drug, then I'll offer up those symptoms to folks with malignant tumors, who are undergoing chemotherapy and radiation and dealing with discomfort far worse than nausea and dizziness.

Or if I have a day where I can't stop crying, I offer up my box of Kleenex to all of my Beyond Blue readers who are treatment-resistant and live too many hours like that.

I suppose this gesture is my small way of attaching some meaning to my aching, so that it does have a purpose after all... like recycling my massive pile of scrap paper and plentiful water bottles...and can better connect me to others who struggle in similar ways.

Untie the strings

A SET OF high expectations is almost always guaranteed to deliver—overnight, no extra charge—a carton of suffering.

I've learned this over and over again when I expect people to understand mental illness: what it's like when your survival instinct ran away with the family dog. When friends and family encouraged me to pitch the happy pills and tough it out like the rest of the world, I came away hurt, angry, and disappointed.

But that was my fault.

Because I expected something.

"Presume no one will understand," my mom used to tell me, "and you will be pleasantly surprised the day someone does."

She was right.

By lowering my standards—both with others and myself—I gave my brain a better shot at optimism and sanity, or at least at not declaring war with the person who simply doesn't get it.

I try to keep my expectations in check today.

When sending an emotionally loaded e-mail, I'll quiz myself, *What's my agenda? What's my expectation? If I don't get the response I want, will I still be glad I have sent this?* Then I visualize myself untying the strings of my expectations...cutting from the little envelope the tiny tails hanging out the sides...so that I can communicate with *practically* no calculation on my part. (A little has to stay to make me interesting.)

Don't force the process

WHEN I'M IMPATIENT to move past a painful period in my life, I remind myself of the process of metamorphosis that happens as a caterpillar becomes a butterfly.

Only in struggling to emerge from a small hole in the cocoon does a butterfly form wings strong enough to fly. As she squeezes out of that tiny space, the liquids inside her body cavity are pushed into the tiny capillaries in the wings, where they harden. Should you try to help a butterfly by tearing open the cocoon, the poor thing won't sprout wings. Or if she does, they would be too weak to fly.

I like to give my caterpillar an enema when I'm transitioning to what I hope will be a better place. I try to force the process however I can. But I do think there is some wisdom in putting the tweezers or enema away and letting nature handle it the way it's supposed to.

Apply some color

LIKE MANY FOLKS raised in an alcoholic home, my thoughts tend to run black and white...lots of zebra thinking. But the good news is that I can always add a bit of color to my sterile surroundings. By simply recognizing my distorted all-or-nothing thinking pattern, I can add violet, peach, and fuchsia to a troubling circumstance. That is, I can see a situation with more options than yes or no.

My therapist helps me to take my blinders off so that I can see for myself that my problems are not black and white. In fact part of the fun, so they say, is learning to appreciate all the nuances—the five shades of purple—in a relationship, circumstance, or condition, and to tolerate the messiness a bit more, like my kids do.

100

Don't be a cooking frog

A THERAPIST FRIEND of mine, Elvira Aletta, recently reminded me of the lesson of the cooking frog: You put a frog in a pot of boiling water, and he jumps out to preserve his life. You put the same frog in cold water, turning up the heat gradually, and he stays in there...acclimating to the temperature. Until, that is, he boils to death.

My pot?

The ice cubes melted when the housing market accidentally fell into the toilet with the rest of the economy, and the world had no need for architects like my husband. I manically pursued a handful of jobs that I've been juggling as gracefully as a Cirque du Soleil dude who got fired for tripping. Yada yada yada through a dozen or so illnesses I've recently contracted, and there I am. Sitting in the pot, thinking to myself, *It sure does feel warm in here...Nah, I'm probably imagining it!*

Alas. It's time to leap out.

101

Learn the alphabet

AS AN ADULT child of an alcoholic with major codependency issues, I got a late start learning the alphabet: that the vowel *I* comes well before the vowel *U*...that a person must take care of herself before trying to help someone else or the world. It's the same logic that flight attendants use when they swear to you that your plane isn't going to crash, but in the event that it does, you'd be smart to fasten your own oxygen mask before helping the kiddies.

Do it in reverse, and you'll all run out of air.

Preserve your willpower

MANAGING YOUR EMOTIONS is like being on a permanent diet. If you start off eating celery with hummus for lunch every day, your diet will last approximately six days. At least that's when I threw out the bag of celery and reached for a BLT.

No. You have to pace yourself—throw in a small piece of dark chocolate...or a pound—so that you keep the momentum of eating right.

Science supports my claim here: Humans have a limited amount of willpower. It's like coal. So don't even try to quit smoking when you're eating veggies, or abstain from your Pinot Noir if you're de-cluttering your house.

One character defect at a time, please.

Your spouse will thank me if you listen.

103

Schedule the obsession

WHEN I GET to a point where my worries are crowding out all the other gray matter in my brain, and I can't seem to have a thought independent of this worry-family, I simply take out my calendar and make a date with anxiety. That is, I pencil in at 7 PM for the next two nights, or however long I need, a fifteen-minute appointment with my fears. That way, if the worries pop up at 1 PM and 1:05 and 1:10, I can say to my brain—much like Katherine's and David's teachers say to me when I try to sneak a parent–teacher meeting fifteen minutes before my slot—"Oh, I'm so sorry, but you are going to have to wait until seven tonight because I have other obligations until then."

The worries don't always listen, of course. They try to climb through the windows of my brain, sneak in through my nostrils, hide like pollen on my hair. But if I keep on training them to not bother me until 7 PM, at which time they can throw a wild bash, then they are more apt to leave me alone during the day.

104

Rip the tags off

HERE'S A TELLTALE sign of a noncommitter: a closet full of dresses and pants with the tags still on. Because by snipping off a sales tag, you are essentially taking a stand on life, making a decision to wear the dress in public; you lose the option of returning the dress. And noncommitters adore possibilities and choices.

I try to rip off as many tags as I can today because I know, by experience, that having a cool wardrobe of never-worn skirts—of blowing off invitations to socialize with and meet fellow moms, neighbors, bloggers—further propels me down the depression hole. When I want so badly to isolate and build a nice, comfy fort in life like the ones out of chairs and blankets David and Katherine build in our family room, I've got to get out the scissors, cut the tags off, and show up for that coffee hour that I committed to. I have to take a chance on the dress and invest myself into my community.

105

Love the questions

THERE IS A reason why I preferred math to English in primary school and high school: Nothing in math is open to interpretation.

No arguments about proper exegesis.

No theories about symbolism or any of that confusing crap.

With calculus, algebra, or arithmetic, there is one answer and you either know it or you don't.

But life is like literature. Where the answer—if there is one—depends on what your teacher ate for dinner the night before or how late her husband returned from work. Which is why we have to befriend the questions and the ambiguity and all the gray matter crowding our prefrontal cortex—the sophisticated part of our brain. For instructions on how to do that, I often turn to this quote by the poet Rainer Maria Rilke:

> Have patience with everything unresolved in your heart and try to love the questions themselves. Don't search for the answers, which could not be given to you now, because you would not be able to live them. And the point is to live everything. Live the questions now. Perhaps then, someday far in the future, you will gradually, without even noticing it, live your way into the answer.

Remember the First Noble Truth

MY FRIEND'S MOTTO is "Life is crap." I used to think this was rather sad and depressing until I realized that she smiled more than all of my other friends combined.

And they were pros at positive thinking.

"The way I see it," she explained to me one day, "is that if you wake up thinking that life sucks, then it can only get better from there!"

Perhaps this devout Catholic was a Buddhist in her former life.

Because she had mastered the First Noble Truth of Buddhism: "Life means suffering."

In their book *Joyful Wisdom: Embracing Change and Finding Freedom,* authors Yongey Mingyur Rinpoche and Eric Swanson explain the First Noble Truth this way:

> If we understand suffering as the basic condition of life, we're better prepared for the various discomforts we're likely to encounter along the way. Cultivating understanding of this sort is a bit like mapping the route of a journey. If we have a map, we have a better idea of where we are.

So here's your assignment. Repeat to yourself the following three words: *Life is crap.*

107

Wait a second or three

PSYCHOLOGIST AND MENTAL health blogger Elisha Goldstein describes mindfulness as a way to "increase that space between what triggers us and the way we respond to it." If we can do this, says Goldstein, we can break out of our "habitual patterns of the mind" and choose a different way, a better way, that will decrease our stress and promote more health and well-being.

It's like counting the seconds between lightning and thunder.

So, theoretically, once I listen to an angry voice mail or receive a discouraging piece of news, I start counting: *one one-thousand, two two-thousand* . . . and see how far I can get before breaking into hysteria. When I'm able to squeeze in at least five seconds between the event and my reaction, I can respond more appropriately and appear more . . . um . . . chemically balanced.

Know thyself

RIGHT AFTER DAVID was born, I tried to become a block builder: one of those moms who loved spending hours upon hours building blocks with her child, with an occasional trip to the kitchen to make organic carrot baby food.

I sat down on the floor and tried to focus on nothing but my Gerber baby and his green snot while thinking, *You sure as hell better be enjoying this because everyone says it goes by so quickly and they would kill to get back here.* But here's my confession: My mind was usually on something else. I could never completely stop thinking about article topics and book projects.

I came away restless and discontent, finding the blocks... well, blockheaded. And I couldn't attend playdates without an idea pad in my pocket, so that my mind didn't have to totally shut down while we were watching Baby Einstein and singing "The Wheels on the Bus." I often left these groups feeling more mashed up than the organic baby food.

"You have to know yourself," my therapist would tell me, "and you're not a terrible person just because you aren't a baby person."

Phew.

She was right.

The bigger the shoe size my kids wear, the more interesting they have become to me, and the more fun I'm having. My smile isn't as forced as often as when they were babies. Their curious minds fascinate me with all the unexpected conversations we have, like yesterday's:

"Mom, why are boys better drivers than girls?"

"Who told you that?

"Did Dad tell you that?"

I still have those days, though—like when chaperoning a group of 105 seven-year-olds to the science museum—when I forget I'm not a block builder and come away feeling as fragile and lifeless as those dinosaur bones at the exhibit. But then I remind myself of my strengths, which apparently don't include driving, and somehow things even out.

As long as I don't have to sing "Wheels on the Bus."

109

Begin again

THE ONE THOUGHT that gives me the courage to type unto a blank page is this: I can always begin again. And on those days that I break every single rule I came up with to maintain better personal boundaries, achieve a sense of harmony in my neurotic world, balance work and home like a veteran cocktail waitress taking orders from a table of perverts...guess what? Tomorrow is a new day.

A blank screen.

My errors from the day before don't matter.

They're gone.

I can begin again.

In other words, even in the valley of disappointments and frustration and sadness lie a few seeds of possibility. There is always a chance, a promise, of growth.

110

Err on the side of compassion

YOU WANT YOUR relationships to last longer than five years? Try this advice from my spiritual mentor and foster dad, Mike: "It's more important to be peaceful and happy than it is to be right."

I often argue with a relative as if we were in court: "Objection, sir! Objection!"

But loving relationships don't operate like a Judge Judy show. They're often lopsided, with one person doing the majority of giving and forgiving, welcoming the other person home like the father of the prodigal son, who had squandered his fortune in prostitution.

You can pursue fairness and equality—spending a chunk of your afternoon counting kindnesses like beans—or you can invest your time into loving a person in the fullest way possible, even if she can't repay you or love you back as well.

111

Swap "if only" for "next time"

A PRIEST FRIEND of mine, Andy Costello, gave an excellent homily the other day about his therapist friend who had been in practice for more than twenty-five years. The therapist realized after so many years of talking to people about their problems that miserable people liked to repeat two words... *if only*. But they could begin a path to happiness if they exchanged *if only* for another two words, *next time*.

One of my first therapists didn't use those four words, per se, but she did constantly remind me that my past didn't have to determine my future, so it wasn't all that productive to dwell on it.

As proof of her theory, she mentioned Oprah, who was sexually abused as a child. I'm sure the talk-show queen has run across the same brain research as I have that suggests neglect and abuse in early ages can permanently program the brain for a lifetime of suffering, but it didn't seem to stop her from chasing after her dreams and pursuing a life of happiness.

Maybe the difference is that instead of saying "if only," she continued to say, "next time." Like to the annoying guest who talked well into the commercials, "Next time we won't have you on the show."

112

Trust your gut

I'VE HEARD THIS in therapy, in support group meetings, from my mom, and from my smarter friends: Never *ever* bequeath your authority to a person not named "I," "me," or "self." When a doctor hands you a prescription for a drug you haven't heard of, research it before popping it in your mouth. Or when a Blockbuster Video employee insists you pay $543 to replace their copy of *Finding Nemo*, buy a copy at Best Buy for $9.99 and hand it to him with a smile.

Scam me once, shame on you. Scam me twice, shame on me.

113

Consider the facts

HAVE YOU EVER crafted a juicy plot in your head, based on complicated characters, intriguing scenes, and complex situations...blanking on the small detail that none of them is real or has happened? I can, at times, talk myself into believing that I am the world's laziest mom, most annoying blogger, cruelest daughter, bitchiest wife, and most self-absorbed and irresponsible friend.

Our perceptions aren't always accurate.

Thank God.

Especially when we're in the depression tunnel and our brain feels like it's in a science lab again.

For example, during a depression, it's not uncommon to curse your boss as Satan's CEO and consider filing for divorce because you're sure that your spouse is the problem, only to emerge from the tunnel a few days, weeks, or months later to realize that your husband definitely needs to stay and your boss is actually more decent than the ones your friends gripe about. That's why therapists often advise their clients to not make any big decision while severely depressed. You simply can't see the real picture.

Better to just stick with the facts.

Take down the empirical evidence in front of you before making dangerous allegations that could seriously screw up your life.

114

Keep the faith

ACCORDING TO A recent *Time* magazine article, a significant body of research suggests that faith improves health. People who skip church on Sundays have twice the risk of dying over the next eight years than the crowd eating doughnuts in the basement after services.

Never mind the doughnuts.

One study shows that church attendance can add two to three years to your life. This is good news...if you're not depressed. If you *are* depressed, it helps to think of faith as Helen Keller once defined it: "a dynamic power that breaks the chain of routine... a safeguard...against cynicism and despair."

I think Keller means that faith doesn't have to involve genuflecting or singing "Alleluia" in a crowd of early risers. It could also mean sitting up in bed, putting one foot on the floor, then the other, and standing up, trusting that some benevolent presence is watching over you and won't let you fall. Or, if you do fall, that the same benevolent presence will catch you and help you begin the process all over again.

115

Don't mistake intensity for intimacy

SOME STUDIES INDICATE that more than half of people suffering from mental illness also struggle with some form of substance abuse. That's not surprising to me since intoxication can often provide a blissful relief...however temporary...to the pain that a depressed person feels.

But the high is deceptive.

In his book *The Addictive Personality*, Craig Nakken writes: "Intensity...is not intimacy, though addicts repeatedly get them mixed up. The addict has an intense experience and believes it is a moment of intimacy." Those two lines helped me to understand the perilous cycles of addiction in my life—and not just to alcohol—in their proper contexts: The intense high that these addictions provide is not a substitute for the intimacy in my life that has taken me years to cultivate and nurture. The high is just a manipulative anesthesia, tricking you into believing that your object of addiction is all you need to live the rest of your life pain-free.

Be cool to the pizza dude

ONE OF MY favorite essays in the collection of *This I Believe* commentaries on NPR is Sarah Adams's piece called "Be Cool to the Pizza Dude."

Her essay articulates a philosophy that I've held since I was sixteen, a waitress at Ponderosa: You can tell so much about a person by the way he or she treats the pizza delivery boy. Actually, by the way he or she talks to all waiters and waitresses. I think that every person should be required, at one point or another in life, to wait tables or be a pizza delivery person.

Because it's a crash course in humility.

And once you have been there, wearing the red baseball cap or the hideous polyester yellow uniform, getting yelled at by a jackass, you make a promise with yourself that you will never *ever* treat a human being the way the jerk has treated you.

Sarah Adams writes:

Coolness to the pizza delivery dude is a practice in humility and forgiveness. I let him cut me off in traffic, let him safely hit the exit ramp from the left lane, let him forget to use his blinker without extending any of my digits out the window or toward my horn because there should be one moment in my harried life when a car may encroach or cut off or pass and I let it go. Sometimes when I have become so certain of my ownership of my lane, daring anyone to challenge me, the pizza dude speeds by in his rusted Chevette. His pizza light atop his car glowing like a beacon reminds me to check myself as I flow through the world.

Check yourself. How are you doing with your compassion and your humility? Do you need to go back and wait tables or drive the pizza car?

117

Greet your inner loser

WRITER JOHN CLOUD of *Time* magazine recently reported on new research that suggests it might be better to simply accept our shortcomings than to deny them or try to change them with a bunch of fruity affirmations.

Thank you Jesus.

Because I've done it the other way ... with the affirmations ... and the result was a self-doubting person who now, on top of hating herself, was also reciting cheesy proclamations to herself like a real crazy. That's right, for close to thirty-nine years, I looked into the mirror and said to the wimpy person staring back at me: "You are attractive. You are smart. You are well liked." And the mirror spit back something similar to Snow White's and replied, "Bite me."

Now, I *have* made progress on my below-sea-level self-esteem, but (confession here) it's mostly because of other people's faith in me: my good friends who called me every day of my eighteen-month suicidal depression and expressed something they liked about me; my loving husband who didn't leave me during that time; my dear mentor who convinced me, after months and months of my insecurity complex, that my writing didn't totally suck. They all had to teach me how to love me.

The new study, published in the journal *Psychological Science*, showed that people with low self-esteem didn't feel better after a series of forced affirmations. In fact, they felt worse than the members of the control group who were spared the affirmations. The study backed new forms of psychotherapy that encourage folks to accept their negative feelings rather than fight them.

So, if you feel like an idiot, don't try to convince yourself that you're not an idiot. Grab a *good* friend and extract the truth out of him. If he says you're an idiot, then sit down with your inner idiot and have some cookies and tea. Give him a hug.

Go to your safe place

I KNOW A "happy place" sounds corny, something Jerry Seinfeld would have a little fun with: "I'm almost there... Can't find any parking... Wait, I just secured a handicap sticker..."

But there's some legitimate wisdom here. In *Home Coming*, John Bradshaw explains a technique for swapping traumatic scenes from our childhood with happy ones from our adulthood. He says that our lives are filled with old anchors, the result of neurologically imprinted experiences that we keep replaying when a situation resembles our childhood. However, with some meditation and what he calls *anchoring*, "We can change the painful memories from childhood by putting them together with actual experiences of strength acquired in our adult lives."

The first step to do this is to create a happy place, where you re-experience those moments in your life when you were accepted, welcomed, and loved, and you swap them for the bad memories. Most of my happy places are outside—the majority of them involve water, because I believe the body's first memory was in the watery womb, where we first learned about the powerful combination of hydrogen and oxygen. But I did designate one corner of my home as my happy place. There I greet my inner child, give her some snacks, and strongly nudge her to release her fears so that she can grow up to be normal.

119

Pin the anxiety on the unrealistic expectation

ONE OF THE most important exercises in my recovery program is a strategy I call "Pin the Anxiety on the Unrealistic Expectation." Usually with the help of my therapist—or in the ten minutes I have right before I get the welcome wave into her office—I will jot down irrational goals like "penning a *New York Times* best seller in my half hour of free time in the evening," "being homeroom mom to thirty-one kids and chaperoning every field trip while being the primary breadwinner for the family," and "training for a triathlon with a busted hip."

Then my therapist and I arrive at some realistic options, like "writing an adequate blog," "aiming to chaperone two field trips a year," and "swimming and running a few times a week but saving the triathlon for after retirement." These goals don't sound as sexy on paper as the overachiever's, but they are friends with sanity, and that's all I care about.

120

Journal

TRY PUTTING YOUR emotions to the page. In an August 2003 issue of *Australian Journal of Psychology*, University of Texas psychologist James W. Pennebaker summarized dozens of studies linking expressive writing to improvements in immunity, academic performance, social behavior, and mental health. In a 2003 British Psychological Society study, results indicated that writing about emotions might even speed the healing of physical wounds.

If journaling about pain can heal your knee scab, think about what writing might do for your heart, mind, and soul! Articulating my journey from the abyss of severe depression and back has certainly contributed to sanity in my life, and I can vouch for others, as well.

Start counting backward

I THINK FINDING your inner Rain Man is a good idea if you struggle with anxiety like I do. You don't have to count straws or toothpicks. But counting, in general, will calm you down.

How do I know?

Because I have always felt much more relaxed after swimming laps for an hour as opposed to running for an hour. Why is that? When I swim, I count my laps (hello...OCD in a swimsuit!), and because I can't walk and chew gum at the same time, I can't really start thinking about anything else while I'm counting or else I lose track of how many laps I've swum, and that's not pretty when it happens after forty or fifty laps.

Michael Breus, PhD, author of *Beauty Sleep*, recommends counting backward from three hundred by threes as a way of quieting the mind. It's somewhat difficult...like swimming laps and counting at the same time...so you distract yourself from all the worries that you would be obsessing about if you weren't counting. Try it!

122

Eat brain food

I'VE TOLD YOU how a limbic system running on pizza, doughnuts, and coffee performs. Not well. So here are some good brain foods to stock up on:

- Spinach! It's full of B vitamins, which help the brain produce serotonin, the neurotransmitter that's real good at sending messages ("I'm happy!") between neurons.
- Walnuts! Apparently rats feel great when given an injection of omega-3 fatty acids. So researchers at McLean Hospital think we will, too! Walnuts and ground flaxseeds are the best non-animal source of omega-3s.
- Milk! Milk products and vitamin-fortified nondairy products contain lots of vitamin D, which increases serotonin production and has been linked to reducing depression according to a study published in the *Journal of Internal Medicine.*
- Salmon! Again, lots of omega-3s in salmon, which must mean rats love salmon.
- Beans! Good for the heart, and the more you eat...the more iron you get, too, which helps combat lethargy and grumpiness.

123

Don't try so hard

RECENTLY I TRIED to win a hula-hooping contest, but I came in last place.

Because I was trying too hard.

By thrashing my hips in opposite directions, I was determined to make the thing stay on my torso. Instead it dropped to my shoes, and there I stood in the middle of a crowd laughing hysterically at my zealous efforts.

It's a good metaphor for life, the hula hoop.

Sometimes the harder we try to make something happen—especially in a relationship or job that's headed south—the more we complicate matters. The more we "insist" on solving a problem one way, the more it "persists" in our life. And when we stop asserting all kinds of false control, we lower our risk for public ridicule.

124

Neuter your emotions

I THINK IT'S my Catholic upbringing that wants to categorize everything in my life as either good and worthy of a halo, or bad and capable of delivering me into Satan's den.

This is especially true of my emotions.

For example, if a friend's memoir makes the *New York Times* best-seller list while my royalty statements continue to show more returns than sales, and I experience a twinge of jealousy, I immediately scold myself: "She's your *friend*, Lucifer. Put your horns away." However, if I simply acknowledge that emotion—not as good or bad, productive or unproductive, feminine or masculine—if I try not to judge it or categorize it in any way, *it* is less likely to make a mess in my head.

125

Make a fist and relax

WHEN PEOPLE TELL me to relax, it has the opposite effect...
especially during an acupuncture session or a gynecologist
appointment, as I'm staring at the beach poster on the ceiling.

I'm working hard on chilling out, so I keep handy these
instructions from the psych ward on how to relax:

Sit up or lie down. If sitting, have your feet flat on the floor
and rest your hands on the tops of your legs.

Make each of your hands into a fist; relax the fists one finger
at a time.

Tighten up each of your feet; relax your feet one toe at a
time.

Loosen up the muscles in your body beginning at your feet
and progressing up to your face. Keep them relaxed.

Close your eyes.

Think of a picture of a peaceful place [for me, a quiet room
with no children or a wooded creek, as long as I don't get a tick
with Lyme disease].

Take a deep breath in through your nose.

Hold the breath for five seconds.

Slowly breathe out through your mouth.

With each breath, think to yourself, *I'm relaxed.*

Repeat the breaths and the thought *I'm relaxed* [or, as I say, "BODY, LISTEN TO ME, CHILL THE HELL OUT"] five times.

If sitting, open your eyes and sit quietly for five minutes.

If lying down, keep your eyes closed and continue lying down [at which point I'm usually snoring].

126

Get a plan

JUST AS YOU can cut your worry in half by educating yourself about the obstacle at hand—tumors, cancer, addiction, depression—you can size off a considerable chunk by getting a plan. It's the second part of the Serenity Prayer: "Grant me the courage to change the things I can."

The week I learned about my blood pressure problem, aortic valve regurgitation, and pituitary growth, I was somewhat paralyzed by anxiety. The color-blind chick in me that surfaces during crises saw two possibilities—life or death—and since she didn't know anything about aortic valves and pituitary tumors, she went with death.

But once I got a plan—once I outlined three basic steps I would do in the next three weeks—my anxiety loosened its grip on my neck and the color-blind gal went off to bother a neurotic friend of mine. That was all it took: three specific tasks that would require the very energy I was wasting on worrying.

One, I ordered two books from Amazon.com on pituitary tumors and the endocrine system so that I could understand exactly what my doctor was talking about and be knowledgeable enough to ask informed questions. Two, I requested my records from both my endocrinologist and cardiologist so that I could review them as well as pass them along to a recommended internist. And step three: I made an appointment with a qualified internist who could help me connect the dots regarding the big picture of my health and help me come up with some preventive measures.

127

Do what's in front of you

ONCE UPON A manic cycle, I produced a list of charities that I wanted to start, all within a few months of one another: collecting food for local shelters, raising millions for persons with inadequate mental health insurance (my family and me). I ran my ideas past my favorite deacon, and he took my hand and said: *"Do what's in front of you,"* meaning that I can't save the world when I'm on the brink of a nervous breakdown myself.

Even Mother Teresa preached this logic. She once said: "It is easy to love the people far away. It is not always easy to love those close to us...Bring love into your home, for this is where our love for each other must start." And Leo Tolstoy has written, "Everyone thinks of changing the world, but no one thinks of changing himself."

Not to say that we shouldn't brainstorm about ways to do good. I very much hope to start a nonprofit one day and raise the money I need to pay my medical bills. But right now, taking care of myself—getting some more solid recovery so I'm not so fragile—and devoting myself to my family is the best way I can make a difference.

128

File the feeling

I'M A HOARDER. At least I've been called one by my darling spouse. But hoarding comes in handy when using a cognitive-behavioral technique I came up with called "file it now, deal with it later."

Sound familiar?

For example, let's say I send a friend an e-mail in which I explain that I'm going through a tough time and could use some extra support. She doesn't respond. My feelings are hurt. At that point, I simply start a file for my emotion and store the data in my filing cabinet until I get more facts.

A month later I send another e-mail or call the same friend, hoping to talk to her about something important, but she blows me off for a second time. I will take out the file and scribble the new information to go with the initial emotion. Finally, when I feel like I have enough data in the file to make a decision about how I'm going to resolve my hurt, I can proceed with the action.

Granted, you don't always need a file.

You might have been born and raised by the logical breed of folks that know how to politely inform their friends that they have done something to *Royally piss them off.*

But with me—and maybe this is true with you—so often I need more information before I appropriately deal with hurt feelings or confront someone. I need a year's worth of transcripts before I feel justified to open my mouth. So, as a hoarder, I capitalize on my strengths, and simply acquire more and more notes until my impressive paper trail is driving me absolutely batty... which, well, takes a while.

129

Locate your buttons

YOUR EX-FRIENDS AND annoying relatives know the fastest way to tick you off. Some may even try to get you running for the door in rage.

But do you know your own buttons?

Take ten minutes right now to identify the persons, places, and things in your life that have an uncanny way of making you...well...explode.

After twelve years of therapy and twenty-one years of hanging out in 12-step groups, I think I have finally located mine: Irish bars loaded with inebriated folks, super-size Wal-Marts with more than a hundred aisles of products manufactured in China, Chuck E. Cheese restaurants with life-size rodents singing melodies to screaming children, and conversations with people who think mental illnesses are like mermaids—not real—and that absolutely every health condition can be fixed with the right thoughts plus a little acupuncture.

130

Be a happy rat

INTELLECTUALLY, I KNOW that I'm supposed to be enjoying the ride of life, instead of rushing to the destination. I recognize the wisdom that Harvard professor Tal Ben-Shahar writes in his book *Happier:* "Happiness is not about making it to the peak of the mountain nor is it about climbing aimlessly around the mountain; happiness is the experience of climbing toward the peak."

But I do think some of us were born more restless and competitive and, well, insane than others. I believe I would belong to this second camp of folks. So I am not going to transform my inner rat into a mellow Buddhist mouse. I just don't see that it's possible. Instead I demand that the inner rodent take a bubble bath or a Valium, maybe both, so that he is a happy, relaxed creature, instead of an anxious, restless one. That way he will catch a little more of what's going on as his four little legs rush off to wherever they are going.

131

Practice, practice, practice

I DON'T KNOW why I would expect sanity to come naturally to me.

Nothing else in my life has.

My career, my marriage, getting rid of some of my post-pregnancy gut—I've had to work hard at all of them.

I make myself run, eat boring salads, and do sit-ups when I'd rather wolf down a medium, deep-dish pizza and devour dark chocolate squares in bed; I clutch my tongue when it's about to say something unkind and clean up the dishes when I'd rather chill out and read the latest skinny on Angelina and Brad; and I sell myself to publishing houses even as I'm convinced I suck at writing and that they'd be foolish to invest in me.

In my humble estimation, acquiring sanity requires discipline more than anything else.

It's about showing up every day for duty, applying one cognitive-behavioral technique after another, playing hide-and-seek with your distorted thoughts until they learn how to entertain themselves, firing up the HappyLite for half an hour every day, working out when you're tired, spilling your guts to your therapist when you'd rather hold secrets, trying to meditate, trying to meditate again, trying to meditate a third time, eating two green things a day, getting eight hours of sleep for a few days in a row, living like a cloistered nun, taking your meds on the good days and on the bad days, and pretending to most people in your life that you're perfectly normal even though all the rowdy voices inside your head scream the contrary.

132

Get your mind out of the gutter

I LIKE TO think of my brain as a bowling alley. Except that my lane has about five gutters, instead of two. They are the neural circuits that determine my mood, and the more I ruminate on a thought—e.g., *I wish I were dead*—the more inclined my brain is to stick to that idea whenever I encounter frustration or sadness.

In other words, the more I go down that path, the wider and deeper the gutter, or circuit, becomes. The good news, according to brain experts like Helen Mayberg, is that by changing the way we process information—by altering our thinking patterns—we can actually adopt different circuits and change the hard matter of our brain.

So let's go back to my bowling lane. When I think, *I wish I were dead,* I've just thrown a gutter ball. No points there... unless I retrieve the ball with a revision to my thinking like *No, Self, you don't want to be dead. You want a reprieve from your pain... so let's figure out how to get one short of a martini and bong hit.*

Then I think, *I'm never going to feel better.* Back to the gutter... rolling along, unless I pick up the ball with a statement like *This too shall pass.*

One last gutter ball: *I won't be happy or whole without his approval.*

Correction: *Now, that's just plain stupid. If you're going to pick someone to play God, at least choose someone with fewer character defects or a little more class. Geeze.*

133

Don't quit five minutes before the miracle

IN THE ROOMS of support group meetings, we remind each other not to quit five minutes before the miracle. I never really knew what that meant until the day I was on my way to Johns Hopkins Mood Disorder Center for a psychiatric evaluation.

I had already worked with six psychiatrists, experimented with twenty-one medication combinations, and tried every alternative therapy out there: yoga, acupuncture, homeopathic remedies, Chinese herbs, magnets, visualization techniques, meditation, cognitive-behavioral therapy.

Nothing helped.

I still wanted to die.

If there was anyone who had a case for giving up on sanity, it was I.

Fifteen minutes before Eric and I jumped into the car to head to the consultation, a friend handed me a copy of *O* magazine earmarked to a story called "The Valley of the Dulls: On Taking Antidepressants." The persuasive piece included several interviews with folks who claimed antidepressants zapped their spunk, flattened their emotions, dulled their cognitive functions, stole their libidos, and crushed all creativity. It was, indeed, the perfect article for a whacked-out chick running dangerously low on hope to read half an hour before meeting a team of shrinks.

I started to shake with anxiety as I read the article.

I almost told Eric to turn around.

I nearly said to him that I had been foolish to hang on to a sliver of hope, that I had been half-baked to think there was any help out there for me. I virtually explained that we had both better face up to the reality that I might be very sick for the rest of my life—unable to work, drive, or care for the kids.

I was so close to giving up.

Literally five minutes before my miracle began.

Surrender to the brain

"SURRENDER TO THE goat"...that's what new mother Sarah had to tell herself to get through the first years of motherhood. It's a hilarious and insightful story told as part of the book *Mommy Mantras*, by Bethany Casarjian and Diane Dillon.

Sarah and her toddler son would walk to the zoo every day, and all the little guy wanted to do was to feed the goat. So they'd stay there for hours...just staring at the goat. Sarah came up with her goat mantra to help her get through the goat hours, embrace her son's particular obsession, and accept the difficult, unique parts of motherhood.

After Sarah's goat story, the authors of *Mommy Mantras* quote Eckhart Tolle: "Whatever the present moment contains, accept it as if you had chosen it. Always work with it, not against it. Make it your friend and ally, not your enemy. This will miraculously transform your life."

My goat is my brain.

There has been many a day that I have tried all of David Burns's fifteen ways of untwisting distorted thoughts, implemented all of positive psychologist Martin Seligman's happy tools, attempted the Spiritual Exercises of St. Ignatius, and still my brain is one big fart. So I merely adopt the mantra "Surrender to the brain" and throw my hands up in the air as I yield to the bizarre thought patterns, the emotional baggage, the neuroses. *You got me, guys. You got me.*

135

Hang on to hope

IF IT WEREN'T for hope, I would be dead. On the worst days of my severe depression—when I confessed to Eric and a few close friends that I was scared to be by myself because the urge to die was too overwhelming—hope saved me. At times it was a mere flicker of light in the blackout of my soul...but it was enough to get me to tomorrow, to keep me alive another few hours.

Hope is about believing in something you can't see, hear, or feel...but that you trust is coming. It's about dreaming of a day in which you'll wake up and be able to taste fresh coffee and a Krispy Kreme chocolate-glazed doughnut. Or aspiring to have an afternoon in which visiting friends won't require an Oscar-deserving performance...an expectation that you will feel again, and love again, and laugh again.

Hope is knowing, despite all evidence to the contrary, that your sadness will one day evaporate and in its place you'll feel joy.

Whenever I fall into the pit of darkness and despair and feel my hope slipping out between my fingers, I remember Meister Eckhart's words: "It is in the darkness that one finds the light, so when we are in sorrow, then this light is nearest of all to us."

136

Believe in redemption

REDEMPTION IS AN odd thing. Because identifying the broken places in your heart and in your life can be one of the scariest exercises you ever do, and yet only then can you recognize the grace that comes buried with every hole. If the journey to the Black Hole of despair and back has taught me anything, it's this: Everything is made whole in time... although not always in the way you think, want, or expect. If you can just hang on to the faith, hope, and love in the people and places around you long enough to see the sun rise yourself, you'll find that absolutely nothing is forsaken, not even those relationships and memories and persons that you thought were lost forever.

So you don't always have to get it right on the first try.

Love deeply

WHENEVER A RELATIONSHIP bomb goes off in my life...
when a loved one has passed away or a friendship has ended
abruptly...and I want to forever retreat to a safe place where I
don't have to trust or love again, I read this favorite quote from
Henri Nouwen and I come out of hiding:

> Do not hesitate to love and to love deeply. You might be
> afraid of the pain that deep love can cause. When those
> you love deeply reject you, leave you, or die, your heart
> will be broken. But that should not hold you back from
> loving deeply. The pain that comes from deep love makes
> your love ever more fruitful. It is like a plow that breaks
> the ground to allow the seed to take root and grow into a
> strong plant...Yes, as you love deeply the ground of your
> heart will be broken more and more, but you will rejoice in
> the abundance of the fruit it will bear.

138

Turn to a cause

DID YOU KNOW that Abe Lincoln lived his whole life with the fear of going insane? Doesn't that make you feel better? Like you're glad you bought this book, just to learn that?

We can learn much from the way Abe got past his fear and anguish to become one of this country's most inspiring leaders.

Joshua Wolf Shenk, author of *Lincoln's Melancholy,* presents Lincoln's three-pronged "blueprint for a successful life with suffering": First he acknowledged his pain. *Yep, it's definitely there. Ouch.* Then he learned how to live with his pain and adapt to it. In other words, drawing from my earlier point, he learned how to dance in the rain.

And finally, he turned to a cause greater than himself. Writes Shenk, "It's not that Lincoln achieved happiness from this, but he did achieve a transcendent wisdom, which was the delicate fruit of a lifetime of pain."

I know from my own life and plenty of others' that turning to a cause, a greater purpose, can transform a series of clumsy falls into a graceful dance, or even a masterpiece. As French Renaissance philosopher Michel de Montaigne said, "The great and glorious masterpiece of man is to live with purpose."

Write a life mission statement

IT'S EASIER TO turn to a cause and to channel your suffering once you have a life mission or, even better, a life mission statement.

For the last three years, I have been helping the midshipmen at the Naval Academy define theirs, a writing assignment for their leadership class. In the process, I decided that I needed one myself. So...

My mission is to educate folks about mental illness and to offer support to those persons, like myself, who struggle with mood disorders, but I do all of this with a sense of humor.

I arrived at this compound sentence after reflecting on Mahatma Gandhi's words, "You must be the change you want to see in the world." The change I want to see? Less stigma associated with mental illness, and more compassion for those living with mood disorders.

I agree with happiness experts that finding one's calling is, perhaps, the most effective happiness booster available because you can assign meaning to your suffering...the pain isn't for nothing. If we don't exit prematurely, the gritty irritants of our shells will eventually produce a precious pearl.

Love the sinner, hate the sin

I AM MERELY using religious language to describe a good psychological tool.

If we can separate what we do from who we are, we are more apt to forgive ourselves and, after a mistake, pick up from where we left off. But if we mix in our mistakes with our identities—tucking them into our coats like I do drinks and snacks at a movie theater because I'm not about to pay five bucks for a Pepsi—then we've got trouble.

For this reason, I have an easier time introducing myself like this at a support group meeting: "Hi, I'm Therese, and I did stupid things when I drank," instead of "I'm an alcoholic." Because there is so much more to me than my inability to throw back a margarita without dire consequences.

Choose a hero

I HAVE A long list of mental health heroes, and I go back and read their stuff or pull out pictures of them on the days when my symptoms make a surprise visit. I pull out a five-dollar bill and remember that Abe Lincoln was suicidal for two years, just like I was, but that he translated his "melancholy"—as they called it then—into a strength that guided the emancipation. I'll pull out Kay Redfield Jamison's memoir *An Unquiet Mind* to remind myself that this famous psychologist is not immune to the symptoms of bipolar disorder. But she continues to persevere, speaking and writing on behalf of those with bad brain chemistry, trusting that she will always have at least a few good days ahead of her.

142

Obsess about what's right

DO YOU EVER find yourself obsessing about what's right in your life?

No. Me neither.

But I think it's possible.

In her book *Train Your Mind, Change Your Brain,* Sharon Begley explains the brain's neuroplasticity: how training your thoughts and flexing your mental muscles can actually alter the physical structure of the brain.

Some simple instructions: Place your insecurity du jour—*X hates me*—in a ziplock bag and store it in the freezer. Next, start preparing some fresh thoughts like *He has every reason to like me, I'm likable, lots of people like me* and place those on a plate for you to consume and stare at, hoping they change your brain.

You don't believe me, do you?

That exchanging *He hates me* for *He might like me, hell I don't know* can change your brain?

Begley writes: "Something as seemingly insubstantial as a thought can affect the very stuff of the brain, altering neuronal connections in a way that can treat mental illness or, perhaps, lead to a greater capacity for empathy and compassion. It may even dial up the supposedly immovable happiness set point."

143

Audit yourself

DID YOU KNOW that it's impossible to feel fear when you're in a mind-set of appreciation?

That's what Dan Baker maintains in his book *What Happy People Know.* He writes, "It is a fact of neurology that the brain cannot be in a state of appreciation and a state of fear at the same time. The two states may alternate, but are mutually exclusive."

So then, to keep from panicking, we have to stay grateful.

How?

Baker has come up with the "Appreciation Audit," a form of meditation where you reserve three to five minutes preferably three times each day to think about something you appreciate. Like your golden retriever (I say this in case you have a day where you don't like anyone else but him), or your favorite kid, or your deceased grandmother who willed to you her baby grand piano, or your bipolar boss who takes his medication, or the Dunkin' Donuts guy who gives you free doughnut holes, or the FedEx delivery dude who leaves doggy biscuits with your packages. You get the point.

You can also do a Top Five list. For example: Top Five Favorite People, Top Five Coffee Shops, Top Five Baristas at Those Coffee Shops, Top Five Ingredients on a Pizza, Top Five Vacation Memories, Top Five Things I Love About My Spouse, Top Five Ice-Cream Flavors, Top Five Reasons I Should Stop Now.

144

Don't forget to have fun

I'LL END THIS book with some of the last words my father spoke to me.

A few months before he died, when I was in graduate school pursuing a theology degree and didn't really appreciate the place of humor or fun in academia, he asked if we could talk about something important. I fretted that he was upset about my B+ in Christology (the study of Christ, not of crystals), but he was thrilled with my grades.

"I'm worried about you," he told me.

"But you just said my grades were fine," I replied.

"No, I'm worried...that you're not having enough fun," he said.

I think about those words every day.

Because, if I were to line up all my neuroses, disorders, and bizarre cognitive patterns, I would say the one that is most threatening to my happiness would be my inability to chill out and have some fun...my propensity to sweat *all* the small stuff and their tiny cousins, making them all HUMONGOUS STUFF in my mind, and thereby leaving no time to laugh. That's why I'm working so hard at flexing my humor muscle and finding ways to enjoy life...so that my dad might look down and be, well, less worried.

Acknowledgments

Ginormous thanks go to Michelle Rapkin, without whom this book would not be in print and its author still dining at Johns Hopkins inpatient psych unit. Many hugs also to Mike Leach, Priscilla Warner, Claudia Cross, Ann and Dick Omohundro, Beatriz Castillo de Vincent, my mom, John Guenin, Holly Lebowitz Rossi, John Grohol, Lisa Biedenbach, Nancy Prugh, Nancy Mascotte, Dawn Staniszewski, Father Dave Schlaver, Deacon Leroy Moore, Milena Hruby Smith, Gretchen Rubin, Carleen Suttman, Caren Browning, Alana Kornfeld, the entire Hachette staff...the editors and copywriters who helped shepherd my manuscript through production and the savvy marketing and sales team who got it into the hands of the bookseller...and of course, the biggest support system in my life: my husband, Eric.

About the Author

THERESE BORCHARD is the author of the hit daily blog Beyond Blue on Beliefnet.com, one of the site's most popular columns. Her blog is published weekly on The Huffington Post and has been featured on Time.com, Yahoo!, CNN.com, *The Wall Street Journal*, *USA Today*, Everyday Health, Revolution Health, Psych Central, and a variety of other websites and blogs. Therese also moderates a vibrant online depression support group of more than seventeen hundred members that was voted Beliefnet's Top Support Group.

She is the author of *Beyond Blue: Surviving Depression & Anxiety and Making the Most of Bad Genes*, and is the editor of *The Imperfect Mom: Candid Confessions of Mothers Living in the Real World* and of *I Love Being a Mom: Treasured Stories, Memories, and Milestones*. With Michael Leach, she is co-editor of *A Celebration of Married Life* and the national best seller *I Like Being Catholic*.

Therese appears monthly on Sirius XM Satellite Radio, is featured regularly on radio programs throughout the country, and has been a repeated guest on national television programs such as *Fox & Friends* (Fox News Channel) and *Politically Incorrect with Bill Maher* (ABC). She lives with her husband, Eric, and their two "spirited" children in Annapolis, Maryland. You may visit her at www.thereseborchard.com.

Notes